D0532104

Children's Illustrated THESAURUS

Written by Sue Graves
Illustrated by Tim Hutchinson

p

US language consultant: Ronne Randall

Designer: Fiona Grant

This is a Parragon Publishing book
This edition published in 2006

Parragon Publishing
Queen Street House
4 Queen Street
Bath BA1 1HE, UK

ISBN 1-40545-018-5

Printed in Malaysia

Contents

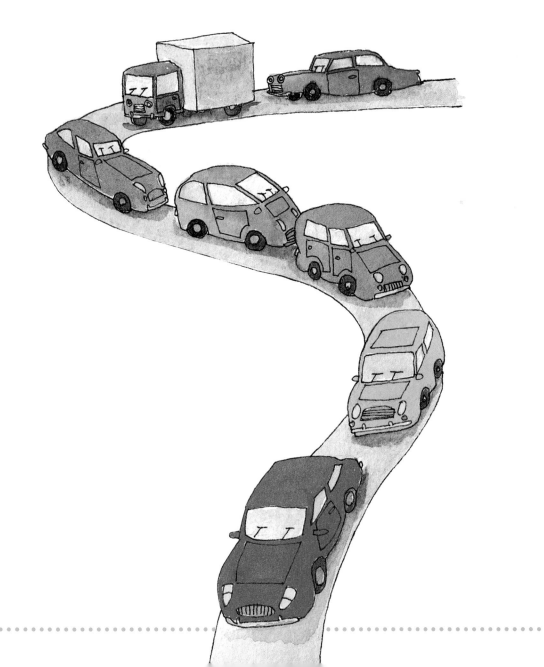

Introduction

What is a thesaurus?

A **thesaurus** is similar to a dictionary. But instead of just giving you the meaning of the word you have looked up, as a dictionary does, a thesaurus gives you a list of other words with similar meanings (*synonyms*). Sometimes a thesaurus also gives you words with opposite meanings (*antonyms*).

A thesaurus is a very useful book. It can increase your written and spoken vocabulary and help you use more interesting words when you write!

Alphabet band
For each letter of the alphabet there is a different coloured band across the top of the page.

Alphabet letter
The letters inside the circle tell you that all the words on this page begin with the letter **b**.

Header word
The word at the top of the left-hand page shows you the first headword that appears on the page. The word at the top of the right-hand page shows you the last headword that appears on the page.

Headword
The headword is the main word that you look up to find synonyms for it. The headwords appear in alphabetical order.

Feature headword
For this headword there are several related words with illustrations that are linked to, but do not mean exactly the same as, the headword. These words will help you develop your writing.

Bb   boast

boast   verb
To **boast** means to talk very proudly about yourself, your things, or something you have done.
*"I am the best wizard in the whole world," **boasted** Mr. Magic.*

1) **brag** 2) **gloat** 3) **show off** 4) **crow**

1) *Mrs. Brown was always **bragging** about her smart son.*
2) *The rich man **gloated** about his big house and garden.*
3) *Sam **showed** off his medal after the race.*
4) *Ella **crowed** when she won first prize.*

boat   noun
A **boat** is a vehicle that floats on the water or moves under it.
*The soldiers crossed the river by **boat**.*

tanker

sailboat

cruise ship

submarine

trawler

canoe

rowboat

speedboat

26

8

How to use this thesaurus

Like a dictionary, words are listed alphabetically in a thesaurus. The word you look up first of all is the headword. After the headword, you can find out what part of speech the word is and what it means. You will also find a sentence showing you how to use the word.

Next, you will find a list of synonyms. These are followed by sentences that show how you might use the synonyms in your writing. If the headword has antonyms (*opposites*), these are listed last of all.

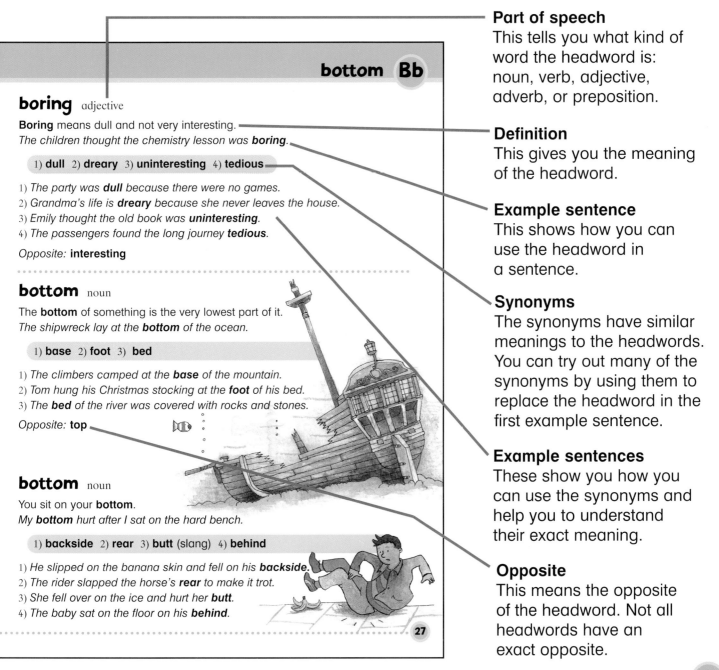

Part of speech
This tells you what kind of word the headword is: noun, verb, adjective, adverb, or preposition.

Definition
This gives you the meaning of the headword.

Example sentence
This shows how you can use the headword in a sentence.

Synonyms
The synonyms have similar meanings to the headwords. You can try out many of the synonyms by using them to replace the headword in the first example sentence.

Example sentences
These show you how you can use the synonyms and help you to understand their exact meaning.

Opposite
This means the opposite of the headword. Not all headwords have an exact opposite.

Content of the thesaurus illustration:

bottom **Bb**

boring adjective
Boring means dull and not very interesting.
The children thought the chemistry lesson was **boring**.

1) **dull** 2) **dreary** 3) **uninteresting** 4) **tedious**

1) *The party was* **dull** *because there were no games.*
2) *Grandma's life is* **dreary** *because she never leaves the house.*
3) *Emily thought the old book was* **uninteresting**.
4) *The passengers found the long journey* **tedious**.

Opposite: **interesting**

bottom noun
The **bottom** of something is the very lowest part of it.
The shipwreck lay at the **bottom** *of the ocean.*

1) **base** 2) **foot** 3) **bed**

1) *The climbers camped at the* **base** *of the mountain.*
2) *Tom hung his Christmas stocking at the* **foot** *of his bed.*
3) *The* **bed** *of the river was covered with rocks and stones.*

Opposite: **top**

bottom noun
You sit on your **bottom**.
My **bottom** *hurt after I sat on the hard bench.*

1) **backside** 2) **rear** 3) **butt** (slang) 4) **behind**

1) *He slipped on the banana skin and fell on his* **backside**.
2) *The rider slapped the horse's* **rear** *to make it trot.*
3) *She fell over on the ice and hurt her* **butt**.
4) *The baby sat on the floor on his* **behind**.

27

able adjective

If you are **able** to do something, you can do it.
*The magician was **able** to do card tricks.*

> 1) **capable** 2) **skillful**

1) *She was **capable** of writing neatly when she tried.*
2) *Jenny was a **skillful** basketball player.*

Opposites: **incapable, unable**

about adverb

About means almost or nearly.
*Jim had **about** four more math problems to finish.*

> 1) **almost** 2) **approximately** 3) **nearly** 4) **roughly**

1) *It was **almost** time for recess.*
2) *The bus was **approximately** five minutes late.*
3) *There were **nearly** 20 children at Jack's party.*
4) ***Roughly** seven children stayed home from school today.*

above preposition

Something that is **above** is higher up.
*The plane flew **above** the clouds.*

> 1) **over** 2) **on top of** 3) **upon**

1) *The walkers climbed **over** the hill to reach the other side.*
2) *The window cleaner stood **on top of** the ladder.*
3) *Mom put seven candles **upon** the birthday cake.*

Opposites: **below, under**

absent adjective

If you are **absent** from something, you are away from it.
*Andrew was **absent** because he had chicken pox.*

> 1) **away** 2) **gone** 3) **missing**

1) *The Jones family was **away** for the holidays.*
2) *There were lots of cakes, but suddenly they were **gone**!*
3) *Grandma was worried because her pet cat was **missing**.*

Opposite: **present**

accident noun

An **accident** is something bad that happens by chance.
*Sam had an **accident** on his bike.*

> 1) **disaster** 2) **crash** 3) **collision**

1) *It was a **disaster** when the school burned down.*
2) *Two big tankers were involved in the **crash**.*
3) *The **collision** took place on an icy road.*

active adjective

An **active** person or animal moves around a lot.
*Our new puppy is very **active**.*

> 1) **lively** 2) **energetic** 3) **vigorous**

1) *The **lively** children ran around the playground.*
2) *The circus acrobats were very **energetic**.*
3) *The boys played a **vigorous** game of football.*

actor noun

An **actor** is someone who performs in a movie or a play.
*The **actor** stood in the middle of the stage.*

> 1) **player** 2) **performer** 3) **star**

*1) The three **players** bowed in front of the audience.*
*2) The street **performer** made everyone laugh.*
*3) The **star** of the movie wore a beautiful dress.*

add verb

You **add** numbers together to find their total.
*You can use a calculator to **add** a list of numbers.*

> 1) **count** 2) **total**

*1) My little brother can **count** up to 100.*
*2) The salesclerk had to **total** the day's takings.*

Opposite: **subtract**

admire verb

To **admire** means to like and respect something or someone.
*The people went to the museum to **admire** the paintings.*

> 1) **adore** 2) **praise** 3) **worship**

*1) "I **adore** pop music," said Donna.*
*2) The teacher **praised** the children's good work.*
*3) She **worshipped** her older brother and his friends.*

admit verb

To **admit** is to accept that something is true.
*The thief had to **admit** that he'd stolen the money.*

> 1) **accept** 2) **own up** 3) **confess** 4) **acknowledge**

1) *Ben cannot **accept** that he is no longer on the football team.*
2) *He **owned up** that he had broken the window.*
3) *I told my brother to **confess** the truth.*
4) *She **acknowledged** that her dog had eaten the food.*

Opposite: **deny**

adult adjective

Adult means grown up or developed.
*Every child had to be accompanied by an **adult** person.*

> 1) **full grown** 2) **grown-up** 3) **mature**

1) *Most cats are **full grown** by the time they are two years old.*
2) *The swimmers were accompanied by two **grown-up** lifeguards.*
3) *The girls in the sixth grade behave in a **mature** way.*

afraid adjective

If you are **afraid**, you are scared or frightened.
*The little girl was **afraid** of the dark.*

> 1) **scared** 2) **fearful** 3) **frightened** 4) **terrified**

1) *Our kitten is **scared** of loud noises.*
2) *The **fearful** knight ran away from the battle.*
3) *The puppy was **frightened** by the big dog.*
4) *The old man was **terrified** of ghosts.*

Opposites: **confident, unafraid**

agree verb

If you **agree** with someone, you think the same as that person.
*Everyone **agreed** that the new building was ugly!*

1) **get along** 2) **concur** 3) **accept** 4) **side with**

1) *Ben **gets along** well with his stepbrother.*
2) *The teacher **concurred** that the math problem was difficult.*
3) *The doctor **accepted** that his patient was sick.*
4) *Lucy always **sides with** Mark during an argument.*

Opposite: **disagree**

aircraft noun

An **aircraft** is a machine that flies through the air.
*A helicopter is a kind of **aircraft**.*

airplane

jumbo jet

airship

glider

fighter jet

hot-air balloon

helicopter

alert adjective

If you are **alert**, you are ready for action.
*The security guard was **alert** as he opened the door.*

> 1) **attentive** 2) **observant** 3) **watchful** 4) **sharp**

1) *Jack is **attentive** and always listens carefully to his teacher.*
2) *The burglar was spotted by an **observant** police officer.*
3) *The soldiers were **watchful** in case the enemy attacked.*
4) *The **sharp** girl spotted the missing jewel.*

amusing adjective

Something that is **amusing** is funny and makes people laugh.
*Mark's uncle told an **amusing** story about his dog.*

> 1) **enjoyable** 2) **funny** 3) **hilarious**

1) *Everyone had an **enjoyable** time at the show.*
2) *The girls watched a **funny** cartoon on TV.*
3) *The circus clowns were really **hilarious**.*

Opposites: **boring, dull**

angry adjective

Angry means cross or annoyed.
*Mom was **angry** when the dog ate her lunch.*

> 1) **annoyed** 2) **cross** 3) **displeased** 4) **furious**

1) *We were **annoyed** because the bus was late.*
2) *Grandad gets **cross** when he loses his glasses.*
3) *The teacher was **displeased** with the noisy class.*
4) *Mary was **furious** when her brother took her candy.*

animal noun

An **animal** is a living creature that breathes and moves around.
*There are lots of **animals** in the jungle.*

monkey

ladybug

frog

dog

snake

butterfly

kangaroo

parrot

seal

shark

annoy verb

If you **annoy** people, you irritate them.
*Joe liked to **annoy** his big sister.*

1) **bother** 2) **irritate** 3) **pester** 4) **tease**

1) *"Don't **bother** me now," said Mom, reading the newspaper.*
2) *The rash on my arm started to **irritate** me.*
3) *The twins always **pester** their mom when they go shopping.*
4) *I **tease** my best friend about her purple hair!*

Opposite: **please**

answer verb

When you **answer**, you say or write something to someone who asks a question.
*"How old are you?" asked the man. "I'm seven," **answered** Katie.*

> 1) **reply** 2) **respond** 3) **retort**

1) *The thief **replies** quickly to the police officer's question.*
2) *The waiter **responded** to our complaint about the food.*
3) *"That's such an awful headline!" **retorted** the journalist.*

appear verb

If something **appears**, it moves to a place where you can see it.
*The ghost suddenly **appeared** in the doorway.*

> 1) **come into view** 2) **come to light** 3) **loom** 4) **turn up**

1) *The ship **came into view** over the horizon.*
2) *The missing documents **came to light** after a search.*
3) *A sinister figure **loomed** out of the fog.*
4) *Michael was sure his missing sneakers would **turn up**.*

Opposite: **disappear**

argue adjective

If you **argue** with someone, you do not agree with that person.
*The boys **argue** about which soccer team is the best.*

> 1) **bicker** 2) **disagree** 3) **quarrel** 4) **squabble**

1) *The sisters **bicker** about whose turn it is to ride the pony.*
2) *My mom and dad **disagree** over silly things.*
3) *When people **quarrel** they often shout at each other.*
4) *Martha and Emily **squabbled** over the remote control for the TV.*

Opposite: **agree**

arrange verb

If you **arrange** something, you figure out how to do something and then do it.
*I'm going to **arrange** a surprise party for my sister's birthday.*

> 1) **plan** 2) **prepare** 3) **organize**

1) *It took a long time to **plan** our safari trip.*
2) *The hotel staff **prepared** the conference room.*
3) *He **organized** a meeting between the parents and the teachers.*

ask verb

You **ask** a question in order to find out the answer.
*The children **ask** their teacher lots of questions.*

> 1) **request** 2) **query** 3) **interrogate** 4) **inquire**

1) *The dentist **requested** that I come back in six months.*
2) *The farmer **queried** what the vet said.*
3) *The police officer **interrogated** the suspect.*
4) *Molly **inquired** whether her neighbor was feeling better.*

Opposites: **answer, reply**

asleep adjective

If you are **asleep**, you are not awake.
The cat is asleep in the easy chair.

> 1) **sleeping** 2) **dozing** 3) **snoozing** 4) **slumbering**

1) *The **sleeping** baby did not make a sound.*
2) *"Shh! The puppy is **dozing**!"*
3) *It is not wise to wake a **snoozing** tiger!*
4) *The **slumbering** giant snored loudly.*

Opposite: **awake**

awake adjective

If you are **awake** you are alert and aware.
Bill was awake all night long because he couldn't sleep.

> 1) **alert** 2) **conscious** 3) **attentive**

1) *The explorer was **alert** as he traveled through the jungle.*
2) *Daniel was still **conscious** after the car accident.*
3) *We tried to be **attentive** in our new teacher's class.*

Opposite: **asleep**

awful adjective

Something that is **awful** is very bad or unpleasant.
Hannah thought her new dress was awful!

> 1) **bad** 2) **horrible** 3) **unpleasant** 4) **ugly**

1) *William's **bad** behavior upset his mom.*
2) *Josh was **horrible** to his sister and made her cry.*
3) *The ice cream had an **unpleasant** taste.*
4) *Litter in the street looks really **ugly**.*

Opposites: **good, nice**

baby noun

A **baby** is a young child or animal.
*The **baby** was only two months old.*

> 1) **newborn** 2) **child** 3) **infant** 4) **toddler**

1) *Mom cuddled her **newborn** in her arms.*
2) *The **child** had a short nap every afternoon.*
3) *Meg was the youngest **infant** in the day-care center.*
4) *The **toddler** played in the sandbox.*

Opposite: **adult**

bad adjective

Bad means not good.
*The puppy was **bad** and ate Dad's shoe.*

> 1) **naughty** 2) **wicked** 3) **evil**

1) *Our **naughty** cat climbed up the apple tree.*
2) *Everyone was scared of the **wicked** witch.*
3) *The magician cast an **evil** spell.*

Opposite: **good**

bad adjective

If food is **bad**, it is not fit for you to eat.
*Tim ate a **bad** apple and had a stomach ache.*

> 1) **rotten** 2) **moldy** 3) **spoiled** 4) **sour**

1) *The **rotten** apples are lying on the ground.*
2) *Mom put the **moldy** cheese in the trash.*
3) *The food was **spoiled** because of the heat.*
4) *No one could drink the **sour** milk.*

bake verb

To **bake** is to cook something in an oven.
*Every Friday, my grandma likes to **bake** cakes.*

> 1) **cook** 2) **heat** 3) **roast**

1) *My dad wears an apron when he **cooks**.*
2) *The chef **heated** the apple pie until it was warm.*
3) *If you **roast** meat slowly it will be tender to eat.*

band noun

A **band** is a number of people who play music together.
*My brother plays the drums in a **band**.*

> 1) **group** 2) **orchestra** 3) **ensemble**

1) *The pop **group** has made a new album.*
2) *There are over 100 musicians in the **orchestra**.*
3) *An **ensemble** played music during the wedding.*

band noun

A **band** is a thin strip of rubber, metal, or some other material.
*Tom wore a red **band** on his wrist.*

> 1) **ring** 2) **strap** 3) **strip**

1) *Mary was proud of her diamond **ring**.*
2) *The traveler fastened the **strap** around his suitcase.*
3) *The nurse put a **strip** of bandage over the wound.*

bare adjective

If a part of your body is **bare**, it is not covered with clothing.
*He stood **bare** with his clothes on the floor around him.*

> 1) **naked** 2) **undressed** 3) **nude**

1) *Babies are **naked** when they are born.*
2) *The pirates were **undressed** down to their waists.*
3) *The **nude** statue was on display in the art museum.*

Opposites: **clothed, dressed**

beast noun

A **beast** is a wild animal.
*A tiger is a **beast** that lives in the jungle.*

> 1) **animal** 2) **creature** 3) **monster**

1) *They saw an injured **animal** by the side of the road.*
2) *The **creature** ran into the woods and out of sight.*
3) *People say there is a **monster** in Scotland's Loch Ness.*

beautiful adjective

Beautiful means very pretty to look at.
*The **beautiful** princess wore a dress of green silk.*

> 1) **attractive** 2) **charming** 3) **fine** 4) **lovely**

1) *The **attractive** girl wanted to be a fashion model.*
2) *The little boy had a **charming** smile.*
3) *The shoes were made of **fine** leather.*
4) *There are many **lovely** flowers in the park.*

Opposites: **ugly, unattractive**

behave verb

To **behave** means to act in a certain way.
*The children always **behave** well at their grandma's house.*

> 1) **act** 2) **conduct** 3) **respond**

1) *The guide asked the children to **act** sensibly in the museum.*
2) *You should **conduct** yourself quietly in a church.*
3) *Our puppy **responds** well when you praise her.*

Opposite: **misbehave**

bend verb

If you **bend** something, you make it more curved.
*A strongman can **bend** an iron bar.*

> 1) **twist** 2) **curve** 3) **turn**

1) *Jane **twisted** her long hair into a big knot.*
2) *He **curved** the cardboard around the glass vase.*
3) *The driver **turned** the handle on the truck door.*

Opposite: **straighten**

bend noun

A **bend** is a curve.
*Watch out for the sharp **bend** in the road!*

> 1) **corner** 2) **curve** 3) **turn** 4) **twist**

1) *He drove around the **corner** too fast and crashed the car.*
2) *The designer drew a pattern with lots of **curves** in it.*
3) *The path took a **turn** to the left by the river.*
4) *The speed camera was hidden by a **twist** in the road.*

better adjective

If you feel **better**, you no longer feel ill.
*Ellen was feeling **better** after having mumps.*

> 1) **recovered** 2) **stronger** 3) **fitter** 4) **well**

1) *He felt **recovered** after catching malaria.*
2) *Beth was a lot **stronger** and able to get out of bed.*
3) *The athletes are **fitter** after training hard.*
4) *Now that Sarah is **well** she can start dancing again.*

between preposition

Between means in the middle of.
*The little boy stood **between** his parents.*

> 1) **among** 2) **amid**

1) *The farmer threw the corn **among** the chickens.*
2) *She heard the boy call out **amid** all the noise.*

big adjective

Something that is **big** is large.
*An elephant is a **big** animal.*

> 1) **large** 2) **vast** 3) **immense** 4) **enormous** 5) **huge**

1) *We take a **large** suitcase with us on vacation.*
2) *The Sahara desert is a **vast** area.*
3) *The king and queen lived in an **immense** castle.*
4) *A blue whale is an **enormous** animal.*
5) *The giant had **huge** hands.*

Opposites: **little, small, tiny**

bird noun

A **bird** is an animal with wings and feathers.
*Most **birds** can fly, but an ostrich cannot.*

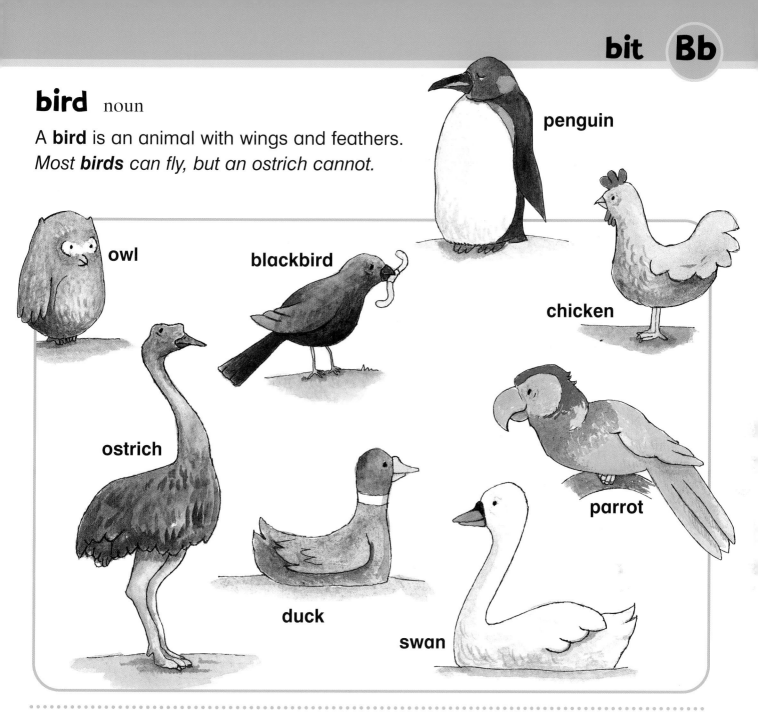

penguin

owl

blackbird

chicken

ostrich

parrot

duck

swan

bit noun

A **bit** of something is a very small piece.
*She passed me a **bit** of her chocolate bar.*

1) **piece** 2) **chunk** 3) **chip** 4) **fragment**

1) *Mom gave everyone a **piece** of birthday cake.*
2) *He had a **chunk** of cheese and some bread for lunch.*
3) *The carpenter knocked a **chip** of wood out of the table.*
4) *I cut my hand on a tiny **fragment** of glass.*

boast verb

To **boast** means to talk very proudly about yourself, your things, or something you have done.

"I am the best wizard in the whole world," **boasted** *Mr. Magic.*

> 1) **brag** 2) **gloat** 3) **show off** 4) **crow**

1) *Mrs. Brown was always **bragging** about her smart son.*
2) *The rich man **gloated** about his big house and garden.*
3) *Sam **showed off** his medal after the race.*
4) *Ella **crowed** when she won first prize.*

boat noun

A **boat** is a vehicle that floats on the water or moves under it.
*The soldiers crossed the river by **boat**.*

tanker

sailboat

cruise liner

submarine

trawler

rowboat

speedboat

canoe

boring adjective

Boring means dull and not very interesting.
*The children thought the chemistry lesson was **boring**.*

> 1) **dull** 2) **dreary** 3) **uninteresting** 4) **tedious**

1) *The party was **dull** because there were no games.*
2) *Grandma's life is **dreary** because she never leaves the house.*
3) *Emily thought the old book was **uninteresting**.*
4) *The passengers found the long journey **tedious**.*

Opposite: **interesting**

bottom noun

The **bottom** of something is the very lowest part of it.
*The shipwreck lay at the **bottom** of the ocean.*

> 1) **base** 2) **foot** 3) **bed**

1) *The climbers camped at the **base** of the mountain.*
2) *Tom hung his Christmas stocking at the **foot** of his bed.*
3) *The **bed** of the river was covered with rocks and stones.*

Opposite: **top**

bottom noun

You sit on your **bottom**.
*My **bottom** hurt after I sat on the hard bench.*

> 1) **backside** 2) **rear** 3) **butt** (slang) 4) **behind**

1) *He slipped on the banana skin and fell on his **backside**.*
2) *The rider slapped the horse's **rear** to make it trot.*
3) *She fell over on the ice and hurt her **butt**.*
4) *The baby sat on the floor on his **behind**.*

brave adjective

If you are **brave**, you are not afraid to do something.
*The **brave** girl dived into the swimming pool.*

> 1) **bold** 2) **fearless** 3) **daring** 4) **plucky**

1) *The **bold** knight rescued the princess from the tower.*
2) *Tom was **fearless** when he climbed the high wall.*
3) *Only Peter was **daring** enough to jump in the water.*
4) *Mom was very **plucky** to tackle the burglar.*

Opposites: **afraid, scared, timid**

break verb

If you **break** something, you smash it to pieces.
*If you drop a glass on a hard floor, it will usually **break**.*

> 1) **crack** 2) **shatter** 3) **fracture** 4) **snap**

1) *The storm was so strong that it **cracked** the ship's mast.*
2) *The falling brick **shattered** the window.*
3) *If you **fracture** your leg you will probably have it put in a cast.*
4) *The batter hit the ball so hard that he **snapped** his bat.*

Opposites: **fix, mend, repair**

break noun

A **break** is a short rest or a change in something.
*We got out of the car for a short **break**.*

> 1) **rest** 2) **pause** 3) **intermission** 4) **gap**

1) *The athlete needed a **rest** after the long race.*
2) *The man took a **pause** from digging in his garden.*
3) *In the play's **intermission** we talked in the lobby.*
4) *The fox squeezed through a **gap** in the fence.*

bright adjective

Something that is **bright** is shiny and gives off light.
*The lights on the Christmas tree were very **bright**.*

> 1) **shiny** 2) **dazzling** 3) **brilliant** 4) **glaring**

1) *I found a **shiny** coin in the street today.*
2) *The stars were **dazzling** in the night sky.*
3) *The **brilliant** diamond sparkled in the light.*
4) *Sunglasses protect your eyes from **glaring** sunlight.*

Opposites: **dim, dull**

bright adjective

A **bright** person is smart and quick to learn.
*Penny was a very **bright** student.*

> 1) **brainy** 2) **smart** 3) **intelligent** 4) **clever**

1) *Bob was so **brainy** that he passed all his tests.*
2) *The **smart** boy thought of a good plan.*
3) *The **intelligent** woman liked doing difficult crossword puzzles.*
4) *The **clever** dog could open the door with his teeth.*

bring verb

If you **bring** something, you carry or move it with you when you arrive.
*I will **bring** your present to the birthday party.*

> 1) **carry** 2) **take** 3) **fetch**

1) *The porter **carried** her suitcase onto the train.*
2) *We had to **take** a picnic lunch on the school trip.*
3) *Dad told the dog to **fetch** his slippers.*

build verb

If you **build** something you make or put it together.
Grandpa likes to build model railroads.

> 1) **make** 2) **assemble** 3) **construct**

1) *Dad is going to make a treehouse for us.*
2) *He tried to assemble the bookcase by following the instructions.*
3) *The builders constructed the new shed very quickly.*

Opposites: **demolish, destroy, knock down**

building noun

A **building** is a place with a roof and walls where you can live, work, or worship.
A skyscraper is a very tall building.

church

castle

mosque

barn

house

windmill

palace

skyscraper

burn verb

If something **burns**, it catches fire and gives off flames.
*The fire **burns** brightly and warms up the campers.*

> 1) **blaze** 2) **flame** 3) **flare**

1) *The fires **blazed** across the forest.*
2) *A match will **flame** briefly and then go out.*
3) *When Mom fanned the fire, the flames **flared** up.*

bury verb

If you **bury** something you place it under the ground.
*Our dog likes to **bury** his bones in the backyard.*

> 1) **conceal** 2) **cover** 3) **hide**

1) *The pirates wanted to **conceal** their treasure in the cave.*
2) *The desert sand has **covered** the ruins of the ancient city.*
3) *Squirrels **hide** their acorns inside tree trunks.*

busy adjective

If you are **busy**, you have lots to do.
*She was having a **busy** day cleaning the house.*

> 1) **active** 2) **occupied** 3) **bustling**

1) *The children spent an **active** day swimming and climbing.*
2) *My brother was **occupied** all day in his bedroom.*
4) *The principal is always **bustling** around her office.*

Opposites: **idle, inactive**

call verb

If you **call**, you shout out for someone.
*"I will **call** your names one at a time," said the teacher.*

> 1) **announce** 2) **cry** 3) **yell** 4) **shout**

1) *The referee **announced** the names of the winning teams.*
2) *"Come back here!" **cried** the dog trainer.*
3) *The coach **yelled** to the players on the field.*
4) *Tom was told not to **shout** in class.*

call verb

If you **call** on someone, you visit that person.
*"**Call** when you're walking past," said the old woman.*

> 1) **visit** 2) **come over** 3) **drop by**

1) *I **visit** my grandma every weekend.*
2) *"Can you **come over** to my house to play?" asked Billy.*
3) *The doctor said he would **drop by** on his way home.*

calm adjective

Calm means quiet and not worried or excited.
*"Stay **calm** while I remove the splinter," said Mom.*

> 1) **quiet** 2) **still** 3) **peaceful** 4) **serene**

1) *The children played a **quiet** game of cards.*
2) *You could not hear a sound in the **still** night.*
3) *Grandpa enjoyed the **peaceful** surroundings of the park.*
4) *The old soldier had a **serene** expression.*

care verb

If you **care** about something or someone, you think a lot about that person or thing.

*"I really do **care** about you!" Jack's worried mom said to him.*

> 1) **mind** 2) **be concerned** 3) **worry**

1) *"I don't **mind** if it rains," said the gardener.*
2) *The pilot was **concerned** that his plane was damaged.*
3) *We were **worried** when Jake arrived home late.*

careless adjective

You are **careless** if you do something without thinking about what you are doing.

*Raul was **careless** with his math homework and made lots of mistakes.*

> 1) **thoughtless** 2) **forgetful** 3) **inconsiderate** 4) **messy**

1) *The **thoughtless** professor forgot to mark the student's work.*
2) *Minnie's grandfather is becoming very **forgetful**.*
3) *Tom could be very **inconsiderate** about other people's feelings.*
4) *"Your work is very **messy**, Andrew," said Mr. Lucas. "Do it again!"*

Opposites: **careful, considerate, thoughtful**

carry verb

When you **carry** something, you hold it and move it with you.
*The builder had to **carry** a large pile of bricks.*

> 1) **take** 2) **move** 3) **transport**

1) *We must **take** the garbage to the dump.*
2) *The movers **moved** the furniture into our new house.*
3) *Trucks **transport** goods all over the country.*

catch verb

If you **catch** something, you take hold of it in your hands.
"Catch the ball, Tom!" shouted the coach.

> 1) **arrest** 2) **capture** 3) **trap** 4) **grab**

1) *The police officer set off to **arrest** the thief.*
2) *The zookeeper tried to **capture** the escaped parrot.*
3) *A spider will **trap** flies in its web.*
4) *Jenny's mom told her that it was not polite to **grab**.*

Opposites: **drop, free, miss**

certain adjective

To be **certain** is to be sure about something.
*Josh was running so fast, he was **certain** he would win.*

> 1) **confident** 2) **satisifed** 3) **positive** 4) **sure**

1) *Dan has worked hard and is **confident** that he will pass the test.*
2) *The baker was **satisfied** that he had baked enough cakes.*
3) *Luke was **positive** that he had handed in his homework.*
4) *The driver was **sure** that the bus would arrive on time.*

Opposites: **doubtful, uncertain, unsure**

change verb

When something **changes** it becomes different.
*My older sister **changes** the color of her hair every month.*

> 1) **alter** 2) **transform** 3) **modify** 4) **vary**

1) *Mom is going to **alter** my new dress because it's too big.*
2) *The decorator **transformed** her bedroom into a princess's palace.*
3) *The general had to **modify** his battle plans.*
4) *Dad likes to **vary** his route to work each week.*

chase verb

To **chase** is to run after someone or something.
Dogs like to chase cats.

> 1) **run after** 2) **hunt** 3) **pursue** 4) **track**

1) *The hungry leopard ran after the herd of gazelle.*
2) *Our cat goes out to hunt for food at night.*
3) *The storekeeper pursued the man who stole his money.*
4) *The guide tracked the elephants by following their footprints.*

chat verb

To **chat** is to talk in an easy, casual way.
Dad likes to chat with our next-door neighbors.

> 1) **talk** 2) **gossip** 3) **converse**

1) *I talk to my best friend on the phone every day.*
2) *Lucy told her sister not to gossip about other people.*
3) *Mom converses with the butcher whenever she goes into the shop.*

cheap adjective

If something is **cheap**, it does not cost much money.
The clothes on sale were very cheap.

> 1) **reasonable** 2) **inexpensive** 3) **reduced** 4) **affordable**

1) *Mom says we can buy the computer game if it's a reasonable price.*
2) *Jasmine bought an inexpensive dress on sale.*
3) *The store had some reduced items after Christmas.*
4) *The builder was selling some affordable new houses.*

Opposites: **costly, expensive**

check verb

When you **check** something you make sure it is right.
*The sailor went to **check** that the ropes were fastened tightly.*

> 1) **examine** 2) **inspect** 3) **test** 4) **look over**

1) *He **examined** the used car very carefully.*
2) *The conductor **inspected** our train tickets.*
3) *Dan **tested** the ocean to see how warm it was.*
4) *The teacher **looked over** the children's homework every evening.*

child noun

A **child** is a young boy or girl.
*When I was a **child** I liked to sit on Mom's knee.*

> 1) **baby** 2) **infant** 3) **toddler** 4) **youngster**

1) *Our **baby** liked to sleep in his car seat.*
2) *The **infant** was learning to crawl.*
3) *She takes her **toddler** to preschool every morning.*
4) *The **youngster** helped the blind man across the road.*

Opposites: **adult, grownup**

choose verb

To **choose** is to decide which thing you want from a larger number.
*Adam wants to **choose** a new color for his bedroom walls.*

> 1) **select** 2) **pick** 3) **take** 4) **elect**

1) *The captain was asked to **select** players for her team.*
2) *We **picked** our favorite toys from the catalog.*
3) *Mom **took** three lamb chops for supper.*
4) *Every year Grade 6 **elects** a class president.*

clean adjective

If something is **clean**, it is not dirty.
*She hung the **clean** towels on the line.*

> 1) **fresh** 2) **spotless** 3) **washed** 4) **scoured**

1) *The villagers took **fresh** water from the well.*
2) *She made sure the house was **spotless**.*
3) *The **washed** tennis socks look very white.*
4) *The **scoured** saucepans were sparkling.*

Opposites: **dirty, soiled, unclean**

clear adjective

If something is **clear**, you can see through it or into it easily.
*The ocean was so **clear** that you could see the bottom.*

> 1) **clean** 2) **transparent** 3) **pure** 4) **unclouded**

1) *The **clean** windows sparkled in the sunshine.*
2) *The florist wrapped the flowers in **transparent** paper.*
3) *I like to drink the **pure** water from the spring.*
4) *The water in the mountain stream was **unclouded**.*

Opposite: **cloudy**

clear adjective

Something that is **clear** is easy to understand.
*The instructions for making the model castle were **clear**.*

> 1) **plain** 2) **simple** 3) **straightforward** 4) **obvious**

1) *The judge told Jacob to tell the **plain** truth.*
2) *I can only do **simple** math problems in my head.*
3) *The **straightforward** directions to the museum were easy to follow.*
4) *Ben finally figured out the **obvious** answer to his question.*

Opposites: **complicated, confusing**

clever adjective

Someone or something that is **clever** is original and imaginative.
*Mark found a **clever** way to store his bicycle.*

> 1) **smart** 2) **ingenious** 3) **quick-witted**

1) *Sam is so **smart** he can name the capitals of all 50 states.*
2) *The **ingenious** entertainer made animals out of balloons.*
3) *The fox was **quick-witted** and escaped from the hunters.*

Opposites: **dull, stupid**

climb verb

To **climb** is to go up something.
*The window cleaner **climbs** the ladder to clean the windows.*

> 1) **go up** 2) **ascend** 3) **clamber**

1) *You **go up** a hill to reach our house.*
2) *They took four days to **ascend** Mount Kilimanjaro.*
3) *They **clambered** up the cliff at the back of the beach.*

Opposites: **descend, go down**

close verb

When you **close** something you shut it.
*The passenger was told to **close** the door behind him.*

> 1) **shut** 2) **fasten** 3) **lock** 4) **slam**

1) *Dad **shut** the front door with a bang.*
2) *We **fastened** the windows before leaving the house.*
3) *The security guard **locked** the factory gates.*
4) *The pirate **slammed** the lid of the treasure chest.*

Opposite: **open**

clothes noun

Clothes are the things you wear on your body. Pants, skirts, shirts, and sweaters are different kinds of **clothes**.

My sister keeps her clothes in a big wardrobe.

pants
suit
shorts
skirt
coat
jacket
dress
T-shirt
jeans
shirt

cold adjective

If something is **cold**, it is not hot.

It was such a cold day that I put on my hat and scarf.

1) **chilly** 2) **icy** 3) **frosty** 4) **freezing**

1) *The sheep stood still in the chilly weather.*

2) *The icy wind blew strongly.*

3) *The children could see their breath in the frosty air.*

4) *Megan was freezing as she walked to school in the snow.*

Opposites: **hot, warm**

collect verb

To **collect** is to bring things together.
George collects all kinds of shells.

> 1) **save** 2) **assemble** 3) **gather**

1) *We **save** glass bottles so we can recycle them.*
2) *The children had to **assemble** outside during the fire drill.*
3) *Every fall we **gather** blackberries to make jelly.*

color noun

A **color** is the way you see something when you look at it in the light.
*There are seven **colors** in a rainbow.*

> 1) **shade** 2) **tint** 3) **hue**

1) *Her dress was a pretty **shade** of blue.*
2) *The painter added a red **tint** to the white paint.*
3) *Mary had hair ribbons of every **hue**.*

yellow: amber, lemon, gold
orange: coral, tangerine
green: emerald, lime, olive
blue: navy, turquoise
red: crimson, scarlet

purple: lilac, lavender, violet
pink: magenta, rose
white: cream, ivory
brown: beige, chocolate, tan
black: ebony, jet

come verb

To **come** is to move toward someone or something.
*Robert asked everyone to **come** to his party.*

> 1) **appear** 2) **arrive** 3) **approach** 4) **reach**

1) *The magician made the rabbit **appear** out of a hat.*
2) *Our friends will **arrive** at 2 o'clock.*
3) *We **approached** the castle through the main gates.*
4) *We **reached** the station as the train was leaving.*

Opposites: **depart, go, leave**

complete adjective

If something is **complete**, nothing is missing from it.
*My dad has a **complete** set of Shakespeare's plays.*

> 1) **full** 2) **whole** 3) **total** 4) **entire**

1) *Sarah has a **full** set of art brushes.*
2) *The greedy giant ate the **whole** cake.*
3) *The **total** bill came to $50.*
4) *The **entire** audience started to clap.*

contain verb

To **contain** is to have something inside.
*This carton **contains** one quart of milk.*

> 1) **hold** 2) **consist** 3) **include** 4) **comprise**

1) *This bag **holds** 30 colored marbles.*
2) *A stew usually **consists** of meat and vegetables.*
3) *The prize **includes** a car and a trip to Florida.*
4) *Our vacation **comprises** a week in Spain and a week in France.*

cook verb

When you **cook**, you prepare food by heating it.
*Every evening my dad likes to **cook** dinner.*

> 1) **make** 2) **heat** 3) **prepare**

1) *Grandma can **make** lots of different kinds of soup.*
2) *Mom **heats** the pizzas in the oven.*
3) *The chef **prepared** a banquet for 500 people.*

correct adjective

If something is **correct**, it is right.
*The cashier gave me the **correct** change.*

> 1) **right** 2) **accurate** 3) **true** 4) **precise**

1) *I gave the **right** answer to the teacher's question.*
2) *The boy gave an **accurate** description of the accident.*
3) *The man took off the mask to reveal his **true** identity.*
4) *This gold watch always tells the **precise** time.*

Opposites: **incorrect, wrong**

count verb

When you **count**, you use numbers to find out how
many things there are.
*My brother uses his fingers and thumbs to **count** to 10.*

> 1) **add** 2) **total** 3) **calculate**

1) *The waiter **added** up our bill.*
2) *The mechanic **totals** the cost of repairing the car.*
3) *The truck driver **calculated** how much fuel he had left.*

cozy adjective

Cozy means warm and snug.
*We were **cozy** sitting in front of the fire.*

> 1) **comfortable** 2) **snug** 3) **warm**

1) *The Davis family lives in a **comfortable** home.*
2) *The baby birds were **snug** inside their nest.*
3) *My thick, **warm** sweater keeps out the cold.*

crawl verb

To **crawl** is to move slowly along the ground on hands and knees.
*Babies **crawl** before they can walk.*

> 1) **creep** 2) **inch** 3) **slither** 4) **wriggle**

1) *The soldiers had to **creep** behind the enemy camp.*
2) *The climber began to **inch** his way along the narrow ledge.*
3) *Snakes **slither** along the ground.*
4) *Worms **wriggle** through the soil.*

creature noun

A **creature** is any animal.
*The blue whale is the world's biggest **creature**.*

> 1) **animal** 2) **beast** 3) **being**

1) *There are lots of **animals** in the city zoo.*
2) *We spotted the tracks of a wild **beast** in the forest.*
3) *Stories from ancient Greece are full of strange **beings**.*

crisp adjective

If something is **crisp**, it is hard and dry.
*The cookies were very **crisp** because we had baked them for too long.*

> 1) **hard** 2) **crunchy** 3) **firm**

1) *The **hard** toffee was difficult to chew.*
2) *Everyone likes eating **crunchy** popcorn.*
3) *The ground at the racetrack was **firm**.*

Opposite: **soft**

cross adjective

If you are **cross**, you are angry about something.
*The passengers were **cross** because the train was late.*

> 1) **annoyed** 2) **angry** 3) **irritated** 4) **grumpy**

1) *The teacher was **annoyed** that the rain had ruined field day.*
2) *The old man was **angry** with the noisy children.*
3) *The fisherman was **irritated** because he didn't catch any fish.*
4) *Jacob was a **grumpy** boy who never seemed to smile.*

cruel adjective

If you are **cruel**, you are unkind to other people or to animals.
*The **cruel** boys kicked the old dog.*

> 1) **brutal** 2) **heartless** 3) **vicious** 4) **ruthless**

1) *The **brutal** man was always in fights.*
2) *The **heartless** thief stole the family's photographs.*
3) *The **vicious** dog attacked the kittens.*
4) *The **ruthless** gangster didn't care who got hurt in the fight.*

Opposites: **gentle, kind**

crush verb

To **crush** something is to squash it by pressing hard.
*You should **crush** the cans before you put them in the recycling bin.*

> 1) **flatten** 2) **squash** 3) **compress** 4) **mash**

1) *The dog **flattened** the flowers with his huge paws.*
2) *Luke had to **squash** his clothes into a small suitcase.*
3) *A huge machine **compresses** the old cars into scrap metal.*
4) *You can **mash** boiled potatoes with milk and butter.*

cry verb

When you **cry**, tears fall from your eyes.
*When Katy hurt her knee she began to **cry**.*

> 1) **weep** 2) **sob** 3) **howl** 4) **whimper**

1) *A bride often **weeps** with happiness on her wedding day.*
2) *Millie **sobbed** because she had torn her new dress.*
3) *The children **howled** when their pet rabbit died.*
4) *Our dog **whimpers** when she hears thunder.*

Opposite: **laugh**

cut verb

To **cut** something is to divide or open it with scissors or a knife.
*The mayor **cut** the ribbon around the new swimming pool.*

> 1) **carve** 2) **chop** 3) **clip** 4) **slice** 5) **trim**

1) *Many sculptors **carve** statues out of stone.*
2) *The woodcutter must **chop** a lot of wood.*
3) *Dad likes to **clip** the hedge to make it neat.*
4) *The chef **sliced** the vegetables with a huge knife.*
5) *I need to **trim** my hair because it's too long.*

damage verb

To **damage** something is to harm or spoil it.
*The storm **damaged** the old oak tree.*

> 1) **destroy** 2) **devastate** 3) **ruin** 4) **wreck**

1) *The flood **destroyed** the old bridge.*
2) *The strong winds will **devastate** the corn crop.*
3) *Sam **ruined** his bicycle when he crashed into a wall.*
4) *The huge waves **wrecked** the tiny rowboat.*

Opposites: **fix, mend, repair**

damp adjective

If something is **damp**, it is slightly wet.
*I'll hang the **damp** clothes on the line.*

> 1) **wet** 2) **moist** 3) **humid**

1) *The **wet** grass sparkled in the early morning sunlight.*
2) *The walls of the old cellar were **moist**.*
3) *After the rains, the air in the jungle seemed **humid**.*

Opposite: **dry**

danger noun

A **danger** is something that is not safe.
*Fred's old car was a **danger** on the road.*

> 1) **risk** 2) **threat** 3) **peril** 4) **hazard**

1) *The man took a **risk** when he dived into the frozen lake.*
2) *The weather forecast says there is a **threat** of rain tomorrow.*
3) *The sailors were in **peril** because of the stormy seas.*
4) *In the winter, ice can be a **hazard** on the roads.*

dark adjective

Dark means there is no light.
*The street was **dark** until the lights were switched on.*

> 1) **dim** 2) **gloomy** 3) **murky** 4) **shadowy**

1) *It was **dim** inside the movie theater.*
2) *The prison cell was **gloomy** and cold.*
3) *It was a **murky** morning because of the thick fog.*
4) *John thought he saw a **shadowy** figure by the wall.*

Opposites: **bright, light**

dead adjective

Dead means no longer alive.
*The **dead** deer lay in the middle of the forest.*

> 1) **deceased** 2) **lifeless** 3) **killed** 4) **departed**

1) *The **deceased** father left all his money to his children.*
2) *The girl carried her dog's **lifeless** body into the house.*
3) *Every year we remember the soldiers who were **killed** in World War II.*
4) *The old man missed his **departed** wife very badly.*

Opposite: **alive**

decide verb

When you **decide**, you choose what to do or have.
*She **decided** to buy the red roses.*

> 1) **choose** 2) **determine** 3) **resolve** 4) **conclude**

1) *I always **choose** vanilla ice cream for dessert.*
2) *Jack was **determined** to get to school early.*
3) *Mom **resolved** to stop eating snacks during the day.*
4) *The doctor **concluded** that her patient should go to the hospital.*

Dd delicious

delicious adjective

Something that is **delicious** tastes very good.
*We ate a **delicious** meal in the Italian restaurant.*

> 1) **appetizing** 2) **tasty** 3) **scrumptious** 4) **yummy**

1) *They found Chinese food quite **appetizing**.*
2) *The meat from the barbecue was very **tasty**.*
3) *"Your home-made pizza tastes **scrumptious**!" said Naomi.*
4) *The children thought that Ben's birthday cake was **yummy**.*

Opposites: **horrible, unpleasant**

destroy verb

To **destroy** means to spoil or to ruin.
*Mr. Jacobs had to **destroy** the letter after reading it.*

> 1) **demolish** 2) **knock down** 3) **ruin** 4) **wreck**

1) *The bulldozer will **demolish** the apartment building.*
2) *The workers had to **knock down** the old house.*
3) *"You will **ruin** your new shoes in the rain," warned Dad.*
4) *The vandals **wrecked** the flower beds in the park.*

Opposites: **build, create**

different adjective

Something that is **different** is not the same.
*The twins like to wear **different** clothes.*

> 1) **opposite** 2) **contrasting** 3) **assorted** 4) **changed**

1) *Meg and her mom have **opposite** views about music.*
2) *Black and white are **contrasting** colors.*
3) *We ate **assorted** snacks at the party.*
4) *Dad was worried about my **changed** attitude to work.*

dig verb

To **dig** is to break up the soil with a spade or a shovel.
*Grandpa had to **dig** the vegetable patch.*

1) **burrow** 2) **excavate** 3) **scoop** 4) **tunnel**

1) *Moles like to **burrow** under the ground.*
2) *The students had to **excavate** the old Roman temple.*
3) *You **scoop** soil out of the ground when you plant bulbs.*
4) *The prisoners managed to **tunnel** underground and escape.*

dinosaur noun

A **dinosaur** is a creature that lived a long time ago and no longer exists.
*Long, long ago, **dinosaurs** roamed over the Earth.*

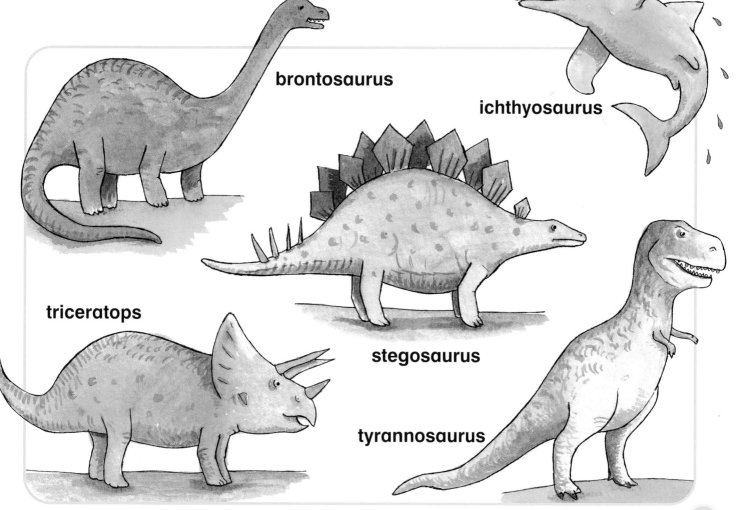

brontosaurus

ichthyosaurus

triceratops

stegosaurus

tyrannosaurus

dirty adjective

Something that is **dirty** is not clean.
*Kate's shoes were very **dirty** after the walk.*

> 1) **filthy** 2) **grimy** 3) **grubby** 4) **muddy**

1) *The rags were **filthy** after I used them to clean the car.*
2) *These **grimy** windows have not been washed for years.*
3) *The children were **grubby** after playing in the yard.*
4) *It was fun jumping in the **muddy** puddle.*

Opposite: **clean**

disaster noun

A **disaster** is an event that causes great loss or suffering.
*The famine caused a **disaster** in such a poor country.*

> 1) **accident** 2) **catastrophe** 3) **calamity**

1) *Tom broke his leg in a skating **accident**.*
2) *The damage from the flood was a **catastrophe** for the islanders.*
3) *It was a **calamity** when I lost my passport on vacation.*

discover verb

To **discover** is to find something or to find out about it.
*Patrick **discovered** some old coins in the backyard.*

> 1) **find** 2) **detect** 3) **unearth** 4) **uncover**

1) *It took ages for Daniel to **find** his sneakers.*
2) *Sherlock Holmes **detected** lots of crimes.*
3) *The dog **unearthed** the bone he had buried.*
4) *The historian hoped to **uncover** some prehistoric remains.*

dislike verb

If you **dislike** something or someone, you do not like that thing or person.
*My mom really **dislikes** spiders.*

> 1) **detest** 2) **hate** 3) **loathe**

1) *I **detest** rainy days.*
2) *The children **hate** it when their swimming lesson is canceled.*
3) *The principal says she **loathes** children with bad manners.*

Opposite: **like**

dive verb

To **dive** is to move quickly downward, often headfirst.
*The penguins **dive** into the water one at a time.*

> 1) **drop** 2) **plunge** 3) **swoop**

1) *The damaged plane began to **drop** toward the ground.*
2) *Jim and Jack **plunged** into the pool.*
3) *The birds **swoop** down to get food from the bird table.*

do verb

If you **do** something, you go ahead with it and finish it.
*My brother likes to **do** his exercises every morning.*

> 1) **carry out** 2) **perform** 3) **achieve** 4) **complete**

1) *The servants had to **carry out** lots of duties in the emperor's palace.*
2) *Our dog can **perform** funny tricks.*
3) *Max **achieved** four lengths of the swimming pool in record time.*
4) *I **completed** the marathon in just under four hours.*

doubt verb

If you **doubt**, you are not sure about something or someone.
*Kelly began to **doubt** that she would get to school on time.*

> 1) **suspect** 2) **mistrust** 3) **hesitate** 4) **question**

1) *The judge **suspected** the witness's account.*
2) *The nurse **mistrusted** our reasons for wanting to help.*
3) *The driver **hesitated** about which road to take.*
4) *The scientists tried to **question** the researcher's findings.*

Opposites: **believe**, **trust**

draw verb

When you **draw** you use a pencil or crayon to make a picture.
*This artist likes to **draw** tropical birds.*

> 1) **sketch** 2) **trace** 3) **doodle**

1) *The art class tried to **sketch** the flowers on the table.*
2) *Ben **traced** the design onto his book.*
3) *My little sister has **doodled** all over my English textbook.*

draw verb

If something **draws** you, you want to move closer to it.
*The movie star always **draws** a huge crowd of fans.*

> 1) **attract** 2) **bring** 3) **entice** 4) **pull in**

1) *Colorful plants in the garden **attract** butterflies.*
2) *The reduced prices **brought** lots of customers to the shop.*
3) *Mom **enticed** the kitten down from the tree with a bowl of milk.*
4) *The opening night of the show **pulled in** a huge audience.*

dry adjective

If something is **dry**, it is not wet.
*Ben put on **dry** clothes after his swimming lesson.*

> 1) **arid** 2) **parched** 3) **thirsty**

1) *Only a few trees grew on the **arid** land.*
2) *The fields were **parched** because it had not rained for months.*
3) *Ted was **thirsty** after playing tennis in the hot sunshine.*

Opposite: **wet**

dull adjective

Dull means not interesting.
*Catherine was reading a really **dull** book.*

> 1) **boring** 2) **dreary** 3) **tedious** 4) **uninteresting**

1) *The children thought the science lesson was **boring**.*
2) *The visit to the museum was **dreary**.*
3) *The play was very long and **tedious**.*
4) *Dad says the newspaper is full of **uninteresting** stories.*

Opposites: **exciting, interesting**

dull adjective

Dull means not bright or clear.
*It was a **dull** day because the sun wasn't shining.*

> 1) **cloudy** 2) **gloomy** 3) **drab** 4) **dismal**

1) *After a **cloudy** morning, bright sunshine appeared in the afternoon.*
2) *The **gloomy** room had only one tiny window.*
3) *The old lady wore **drab** clothes.*
4) *Everyone stayed inside because of the **dismal** weather.*

eager adjective

If you are **eager**, you really want to do or have something.
*The football team was **eager** to start the game.*

> 1) **enthusiastic** 2) **impatient** 3) **keen**

1) *The audience was very **enthusiastic** about the new band.*
2) *The passengers were **impatient** to board the plane.*
3) *Clare was **keen** to practice her ice skating.*

easy adjective

Easy means not difficult.
*We thought the math test was **easy**.*

> 1) **clear** 2) **simple** 3) **straightforward** 4) **plain**

1) *The leaflet gave **clear** instructions for building the model plane.*
2) *The chemistry experiment was **simple** once the teacher had explained it.*
3) *The directions to our new house are very **straightforward**.*
4) *The computer manual was written in **plain** language.*

Opposites: **difficult, hard**

eat verb

When you **eat** you chew food and then swallow it.
*My grandma likes to **eat** eggs for breakfast.*

> 1) **chew** 2) **consume** 3) **munch** 4) **swallow**

1) *Mom told Fred to **chew** his food properly.*
2) *Our dogs **consume** a lot of food each day.*
3) *Horses like to **munch** hay.*
4) *After you have chewed your food you **swallow** it.*

empty adjective

If something is **empty**, it has nothing or no one in it.
*The box was **empty** because we had eaten all the cookies.*

> 1) **bare** 2) **vacant** 3) **unoccupied** 4) **hollow**

1) *The floor was **bare** with no carpet or rugs on it.*
2) *The apartment was **vacant** after the students moved out.*
3) *The old mansion has been **unoccupied** for many years.*
4) *A family of owls lives inside the **hollow** tree trunk.*

Opposite: **full**

end noun

The **end** of something is the last part of it.
*The audience clapped at the **end** of the concert.*

> 1) **ending** 2) **finish** 3) **conclusion**

1) *The crime novel had a really exciting **ending**.*
2) *There was an exciting **finish** to this year's marathon.*
3) *The meeting came to a quick **conclusion** when the protesters walked in.*

Opposites: **beginning, start**

end verb

If something **ends**, it stops or finishes.
*Our school term **ends** at the beginning of June.*

> 1) **finish** 2) **conclude** 3) **stop** 4) **cease**

1) *Matthew **finished** his homework before going out to play.*
2) *The concert **concluded** with a piano solo.*
3) *The rain finally **stopped** after lunch.*
4) *The fighting **ceased** when the police arrived.*

Opposites: **begin, start**

enjoy verb

If you **enjoy** something, you really like doing it.
*Tim and Kelly **enjoy** watching television.*

> 1) **appreciate** 2) **like** 3) **love**

1) *My parents **appreciate** the good food in the Japanese restaurant.*
2) *We **like** to eat outdoors in the summer.*
3) *The twins **love** visiting the local farm.*

Opposites: **detest, hate, loathe**

enormous adjective

Enormous means very big.
*Tyrannosaurus rex was an **enormous** dinosaur.*

> 1) **gigantic** 2) **huge** 3) **giant** 4) **massive**

1) *A **gigantic** wave swept over the ship.*
2) *A **huge** rock fell from the cliff.*
3) *The explorers found some **giant** footprints in the snow.*
4) *Mount Everest is a **massive** mountain.*

Opposites: **little, small, tiny**

enough adjective

If you have **enough** of something, you have as much as you need.
*Mom bought **enough** food to last the whole week.*

> 1) **ample** 2) **adequate** 3) **sufficient**

1) *The greengrocer had an **ample** supply of apples.*
2) *There was **adequate** food for all the children at the school picnic.*
3) *There is a **sufficient** supply of water on the island.*

Opposites: **inadequate, insufficient**

enter verb

To **enter** is to go in or to come in.
*The knights could **enter** the castle through a secret passageway.*

> 1) **come in** 2) **go in** 3) **arrive**

1) *Dad **came in** through the front door.*
2) *The nurse called our names to **go in** and see the doctor.*
3) *The actress **arrived** by the stage door.*

even adjective

If something is **even**, it is flat and smooth.
*The new linoleum was more **even** than the old carpet.*

> 1) **flat** 2) **smooth** 3) **level**

1) *The paper was folded into a **flat** shape.*
2) *The girl had **smooth**, shiny hair.*
3) *A **level** pathway led to the metal gate.*

Opposites: **bumpy, rough**

even adjective

If two things are **even**, it means they are the same.
*Jack and Luke had **even** scores in the math test.*

> 1) **the same** 2) **level** 3) **equal**

1) *Mary and Beth wore **the same** dresses.*
2) *The painting on the wall was **level** with the bookcase.*
3) *The twins were given **equal** amounts of money for their birthday.*

Opposite: **different**

evil adjective

Evil means bad or wicked.
*The **evil** witch stood by her cauldron to cast a spell.*

> 1) **bad** 2) **wicked** 3) **hateful** 4) **wrong**

1) *The **bad** soldiers were punished by the general.*
2) *The burglar was **wicked** to steal from the old lady.*
3) *The cruel man was **hateful** to his old dog.*
4) *It is **wrong** to steal from other people.*

Opposite: **good**

excellent adjective

Excellent means very good.
*Jack got **excellent** grades on his report.*

> 1) **outstanding** 2) **superb** 3) **wonderful**

1) *Emma trained hard to become an
   outstanding rider.*
2) *Lucy played a **superb** game of tennis.*
3) *Everyone had a **wonderful** time at
   my birthday party.*

excited adjective

Excited means happy and lively.
*Our puppy gets very **excited** when we play with her.*

> 1) **lively** 2) **thrilled** 3) **boisterous**

1) *The playground was full of **lively** children.*
2) *The boy was **thrilled** by the magician's amazing tricks.*
3) *Sam and Michael were so **boisterous** that they broke a chair.*

Opposites: **bored, dull**

explain verb

To **explain** is to make something easy to understand.
*The instructor tried to **explain** how to use the new running machine.*

> 1) **clarify** 2) **make clear** 3) **demonstrate**

1) *The manager **clarified** what to do when the fire alarm rings.*
2) *Mr. Jones **made clear** that he expected us to behave well on the trip.*
3) *The chef **demonstrated** how to make perfect pastry.*

extinct adjective

If an animal is **extinct**, there are no more of that kind alive on Earth.
*Dinosaurs became **extinct** millions of years ago.*

> 1) **lost** 2) **vanished**

1) *No one had seen the **lost** tribe for many years.*
3) *Two kinds of Asian tiger are now **vanished** species.*

Opposite: **living**

extraordinary adjective

Something that is **extraordinary** is very unusual.
*Fred's aunt is wearing an **extraordinary** hat.*

> 1) **amazing** 2) **bizarre** 3) **strange** 4) **unusual**

1) *Jim did an **amazing** dive into the pool.*
2) *Todd got a **bizarre** present from his grandfather.*
3) *Our local novelty store sells **strange** things.*
4) *The **unusual** design for the new school building won first prize.*

Opposites: **ordinary, usual**

faint adjective

Someone or something that is **faint** is not strong.
The pictures in the old book were very faint.

> 1) **weak** 2) **pale** 3) **dim**

1) *The summer heat made Grandma feel weak.*
2) *The nursery walls were painted in very pale colors.*
3) *The travelers could see a dim light in the distance.*

Opposites: **bold, distinct, strong**

fair adjective

If something is **fair**, it seems to be reasonable and the right thing to do.
A baseball umpire has to be fair to both teams.

> 1) **just** 2) **equal** 3) **right** 4) **proper**

1) *The prisoner received a just punishment for his crime.*
2) *Mom gave us equal amounts of ice cream.*
3) *Everyone agreed that Jack was the right choice for team captain.*
4) *The jury tried to make proper decisions about the court case.*

Opposite: **unfair**

fall verb

To **fall** is to move downward quickly.
The parachutist started to fall back down to the ground.

> 1) **drop** 2) **descend** 3) **dive** 4) **plunge**

1) *When it's windy the leaves drop off the trees.*
2) *The elevator descends to the next floor in the store.*
3) *The children wanted to dive into the deep end of the pool.*
4) *Kingfishers plunge to grab fish from the water.*

Opposite: **rise**

famous adjective

Someone who is **famous** is well known to lots of people.
*The **famous** pop star performed for her fans.*

> 1) **well-known** 2) **eminent** 3) **celebrated**

1) *Have you ever spotted a **well-known** movie star in the street?*
2) *The **eminent** scientist won a Nobel prize.*
3) *The **celebrated** artist held an exhibition of his work.*

fantastic adjective

Fantastic means absolutely wonderful.
*Beth's new party shoes are **fantastic**.*

> 1) **amazing** 2) **far-fetched** 3) **extraordinary** 3) **incredible**

1) *I'm reading an **amazing** book about dragons and unicorns.*
2) *The science fiction author wrote some **far-fetched** stories.*
3) *The actresses wore some **extraordinary** costumes.*
4) *My uncle told us about his **incredible** adventures.*

faraway adjective

Something that is **faraway** is not near.
*Pluto is a **faraway** planet.*

> 1) **distant** 2) **remote** 3) **outlying**

1) *Dan could see the **distant** hills on the horizon.*
2) *The shepherd lived in a **remote** cottage on the mountain.*
3) *The floods cut off an **outlying** farm for three days.*

Opposite: **near**

fast adjective

Someone or something that is **fast** can move quickly.
*The **fast** cars sped around the racetrack.*

> 1) **quick** 2) **speedy** 3) **rapid** 4) **swift**

1) *I take the dog for a **quick** walk every morning.*
2) *Dad's new car was very **speedy** in traffic.*
3) *The **rapid** train reaches New York in less than two hours.*
4) *The gazelle is a **swift** and graceful animal.*

Opposite: **slow**

fat adjective

Fat means big and rounded.
*Bert is **fat** because he eats too many fries!*

> 1) **plump** 2) **chubby** 3) **overweight** 4) **tubby**

1) *Dad roasted a **plump** chicken for dinner.*
2) *Carl had a **chubby** pig as a pet.*
3) *George is so **overweight** that he can't fit into his clothes.*
4) *Ellie's teddy bear is very **tubby**.*

Opposites: **slim, thin**

fear noun

You feel **fear** when you think something bad is about to happen to you.
*We shook with **fear** when we thought we saw a ghost.*

> 1) **fright** 2) **terror** 3) **dread** 4) **alarm**

1) *Ben gave his sister a **fright** when he jumped out of the closet.*
2) *The scary movie filled the audience with **terror**.*
3) *My mom has a real **dread** of spiders.*
4) *The guard raised the **alarm** when the fire started.*

eel verb

If you **feel** something, you touch it to see what it's like.
*Thick, woolly blankets **feel** soft and warm.*

> 1) **touch** 2) **finger** 3) **pet**

1) *You must not **touch** the displays in the museum.*
2) *I like to **finger** the little stones on Mom's bracelet.*
3) *Kittens purr when you **pet** them.*

ierce adjective

Fierce means angry and dangerous.
*The **fierce** dog barked at the mail carrier.*

> 1) **dangerous** 2) **ferocious** 3) **savage** 4) **vicious**

1) *The hippopotamus is a large and **dangerous** animal.*
2) *The mother tiger behaved in a **ferocious** way.*
3) *A **savage** lion was stalking the herd of zebras.*
4) *The guard dog is **vicious** if you get too close to it.*

Opposite: **gentle**

fight verb

If you **fight** someone, you try to hurt that person.
*The two armies were about to **fight** over the disputed land.*

> 1) **battle** 2) **struggle** 3) **brawl** 4) **grapple**

1) *In olden days knights used to **battle** on horseback.*
2) *The two girls **struggled** over the new CD player.*
3) *The rival gangs were **brawling** in the streets.*
4) *The two warriors **grappled** with each other.*

fill verb

If you **fill** something, you make it full.
*The farmer will **fill** the barn with hay.*

> 1) **cram** 2) **load** 3) **pack** 4) **stuff**

1) *It is rude to **cram** your mouth with food.*
2) *The men **loaded** the furniture into the moving van.*
3) *The dentist **packed** lots of appointments into her busy day.*
4) *Mom will **stuff** the toy horse with a special filling.*

Opposites: **clear out, empty**

find verb

When you **find** someone or something, you come across what
you have been looking for.
*Josh had to search everywhere to **find** his soccer cleats.*

> 1) **notice** 2) **spot** 3) **trace** 4) **discover**

1) *I **noticed** the lost kitten under a bush.*
2) *A stolen car was **spotted** at the end of the street.*
3) *My aunt has been trying to **trace** her long-lost brother for years.*
4) *The walkers had to **discover** the way home for themselves.*

Opposite: **lose**

finish verb

When you **finish** something, you come to the end of it.
*Peter was the last person to **finish** the sack race.*

> 1) **end** 2) **conclude** 3) **stop**

1) *The film **ended** at 10 o'clock.*
2) *The show **concluded** with a big chorus.*
3) *Grandma told us to **stop** being so noisy.*

Opposites: **begin, start**

ix verb

If you **fix** something, you make it work again.
*Katy had to **fix** her punctured tire.*

> 1) **repair** 2) **mend** 3) **patch**

1) *The garage will **repair** my damaged car.*
2) *Dad **mended** the broken desk lamp.*
3) *Grandpa **patched** the broken window
   in his greenhouse.*

Opposite: **break**

ly verb

To **fly** is to move through the air.
*Most birds use their wings to **fly**.*

> 1) **soar** 2) **glide** 3) **swoop** 4) **float**

1) *Eagles **soar** high into the sky.*
2) *The plane started to **glide** toward the runway.*
3) *The gull **swooped** down and caught a fish.*
4) *A feather will **float** slowly down to the ground.*

og noun

Fog is a thick, misty air that you cannot see through.
*He switched on the car headlights in the thick **fog**.*

> 1) **mist** 2) **haze** 3) **smog**

1) *An early morning **mist** hung over the ocean.*
2) *The trees seemed to shimmer in the **haze**.*
3) *The driver found it hard to find his way in the thick **smog**.*

Ff follow

follow verb

If you **follow**, you move along behind a person or thing.
*The children **follow** their teacher into the classroom.*

1) **pursue** 2) **chase** 3) **trail** 4) **track**

1) *The police officer **pursued** the burglar.*
2) *Our dog likes to **chase** cats.*
3) *The private detective **trailed** the chief suspect.*
4) *The ranger **tracked** the animals across the plain.*

food noun

Food is what you eat to stay alive and well.
*Mom bought lots of **food** at the supermarket.*

fruit

bread

vegetables

meat

fish

cupcakes

eggs

salad

66

ice cream

forget verb

If you **forget** something, you do not remember it.
*Do not **forget** to feed your pet every day.*

> 1) **ignore** 2) **omit** 3) **overlook**

1) *Sarah tried to **ignore** the bully in her class.*
2) *The airline **omitted** some names from the passenger list.*
3) *The principal said he would **overlook** Joe's bad behavior this time.*

Opposite: **remember**

free adjective

If something is **free**, you do not have to pay money for it.
*The tickets to the open-air concert were **free**.*

> 1) **complimentary** 2) **on the house**

1) *We were given **complimentary** tickets to the theater.*
2) *The new restaurant owner gave his first customers a meal **on the house**.*

free adjective

If something is **free**, it is not being used.
*The seat next to me was **free**.*

> 1) **available** 2) **vacant** 3) **unoccupied**

1) *The next **available** flight from Chicago was at 2 pm.*
2) *I asked the hotel manager if he had any **vacant** rooms for the night.*
3) *We couldn't find any **unoccupied** seats on the train.*

Opposites: **in use, occupied, taken**

friend noun

A **friend** is someone you know and like.
*Sarah is Rosie's best **friend**.*

> 1) **pal** 2) **companion** 3) **ally**

1) *Tom missed his **pals** when he moved house.*
2) *Mrs. Brown's dog was a good **companion**.*
3) *France and Britain were America's **allies** in World War II.*

Opposite: **enemy**

frighten verb

If you **frighten** someone, you scare that person.
*My friend Josh tried to **frighten** me with a toy spider.*

> 1) **alarm** 2) **scare** 3) **startle** 4) **terrify**

1) *If you jump out at people you **alarm** them.*
2) *The spooky film **scared** the audience.*
3) *If you **startle** a horse it may rear up.*
4) *Big snakes **terrify** many people.*

Opposites: **calm, reassure**

frown verb

If you **frown**, you make an angry face at someone or something.
*The professor **frowned** when the students talked during his lecture.*

> 1) **glare** 2) **scowl** 3) **glower** 4) **grimace**

1) *Mom **glared** at me because my room was so messy.*
2) *The goalkeeper **scowled** when the other team scored.*
3) *The general **glowered** at the soldiers in front of him.*
4) *The runners **grimaced** as they crossed the finish line.*

fruit noun

A **fruit** is the part of a plant that you can eat.
*Most **fruits** are sweet and juicy.*

apples

oranges

bananas

strawberries

grapes

pineapple

pears

peaches

full adjective

If something is **full**, it contains as much as possible.
*The suitcase was **full** of vacation clothes.*

1) **filled** 2) **crammed** 3) **crowded** 4) **packed**

1) *The bag was **filled** with groceries.*
2) *The library is **crammed** with new books.*
3) *The streets of New York are very **crowded**.*
4) *The stadium was **packed** with fans.*

Opposites: **empty, incomplete**

funny adjective

Something that is **funny** makes you laugh.
*Simon told his friends a **funny** joke.*

> 1) **amusing** 2) **comical** 3) **hilarious** 4) **entertaining**

1) *There are some **amusing** cartoons in this magazine.*
2) *The clown made everyone laugh with his **comical** dance.*
3) *Everyone enjoyed the **hilarious** movie.*
4) *"The Lion King" is a very **entertaining** show.*

Opposites: **sad, serious**

funny adjective

Something that is **funny** is a little surprising or out of the ordinary.
*Sam had a **funny** feeling that someone was following him.*

> 1) **odd** 2) **peculiar** 3) **strange** 4) **unusual**

1) *The art teacher liked to wear **odd** clothes.*
2) *We found a **peculiar** shell on the beach.*
3) *Jasmine saw a **strange** car in the street.*
4) *Mom wore an **unusual** hat to my sister's wedding.*

fuss noun

A **fuss** is a disturbance.
*There was a big **fuss** when the cow fell into the pond.*

> 1) **commotion** 2) **uproar** 3) **trouble**

1) *The fire in the main street caused a big **commotion**.*
2) *There was an **uproar** when the concert was canceled.*
3) *Dad made **trouble** when the barber cut his hair too short.*

generous adjective

A **generous** person enjoys giving to others.
*The **generous** boss gave everyone fabulous Christmas presents.*

> 1) **magnanimous** 2) **liberal** 3) **charitable** 4) **lavish**

1) *The **magnanimous** executive gave lots of money to charity.*
2) *The teacher was very **liberal** with his time.*
3) *The oil company gave **charitable** gifts to good causes.*
4) *Amy's mother was **lavish** with her praise.*

gentle adjective

Someone who is **gentle** is soft and kind.
*The **gentle** girl picked up the kitten.*

> 1) **soft** 2) **mild** 3) **tender**

1) *The announcer spoke in a **soft** voice.*
2) *There was a **mild** breeze at the coast.*
3) *Hannah gave her puppy a **tender** pat.*

Opposites: **harsh, rough**

get verb

If you **get** something, you receive it or have it.
*Jess hopes to **get** a new bike for her birthday.*

> 1) **acquire** 2) **obtain** 3) **earn** 4) **receive**

1) *Alison **acquired** her grandmother's jewels.*
2) *Everyone wants to **obtain** the latest computer games.*
3) *I am going to **earn** a lot of money by babysitting.*
4) *Jenny **received** a new book from her aunt.*

Opposite: **lose**

gift noun

A **gift** is a present that someone gives to you.
*Robert could not wait to open his **gift**.*

> 1) **present** 2) **donation** 3) **bonus**

1) *Her birthday **present** was a new dress.*
2) *The electronics company gave a big **donation** to the famine appeal.*
3) *The employees got a **bonus** from their boss.*

give verb

To **give** means to let someone have something.
*Dad likes to **give** Mom flowers on her birthday.*

> 1) **grant** 2) **present** 3) **donate** 4) **provide**

1) *The good fairy **granted** three wishes to the princess.*
2) *The referee **presented** the prize to the winning team.*
3) *We were asked to **donate** money to the charity.*
4) *The teacher **provided** us with the answers.*

Opposites: **receive, take**

glad adjective

If you are **glad**, you are pleased and happy.
*I'm **glad** that my favorite cousin is coming to stay.*

> 1) **pleased** 2) **delighted** 3) **happy** 4) **joyful**

1) *Dan was **pleased** with his new skateboard.*
2) *Grandma was **delighted** to see all her grandchildren.*
3) *The children had a **happy** vacation at the beach.*
4) *Ellie wished all her friends a very **joyful** Christmas.*

Opposites: **sad, unhappy**

glow noun

A **glow** is a warm shine.
The hotel dining room had a warm, welcoming glow.

> 1) **glimmer** 2) **radiance** 3) **shine**

1) *There was a **glimmer** in the singer's eyes.*
2) *Everyone noticed the bride's **radiance** on her wedding day.*
3) *James polished his shoes to give them a **shine**.*

go verb

To **go** is to move toward or away from something.
Mom said it was time to go to bed.

> 1) **depart** 2) **leave** 3) **set off**

1) *The train will **depart** from platform six.*
2) *We had to **leave** the house at three o'clock.*
3) *My parents **set off** for the beach.*

Opposites: **remain, stay**

go noun

To give something a **go** means to try it.
Last year I gave skateboarding a go.

> 1) **try** 2) **effort** 3) **attempt**

1) *Dad persuaded me to give football a **try**.*
2) *We made an **effort** to play our new board game.*
3) *The archer hit the bullseye on the first **attempt**.*

good adjective

If you are **good** you behave well.
*She was a **good** girl at the party.*

> 1) **well behaved** 2) **polite** 3) **virtuous** 4) **obedient**

1) *The class was **well behaved** on the school trip.*
2) *Peter was a **polite** boy.*
3) *King Frederick was a **virtuous** ruler.*
4) *Laura has a very **obedient** dog.*

Opposite: **naughty**

good adjective

If something is **good**, it is of the best quality.
*We watched a **good** movie last night.*

> 1) **excellent** 2) **super** 3) **first class** 4) **splendid**

1) *The pianist was an **excellent** musician.*
2) *Mom cooked a **super** meal.*
3) *The TV show was **first class**.*
4) *Michael made a **splendid** model of a monster.*

Opposite: **bad**

grab adjective

If you **grab** something, you take it quickly.
*The thief tried to **grab** my purse.*

> 1) **seize** 2) **take** 3) **snatch** 3) **pluck**

1) *The captain tried to **seize** the stowaways.*
2) *The pirates **took** the treasure and sailed away.*
3) *It is rude to **snatch** when someone hands you something.*
2) *The sailor leaned over the side to **pluck** the girl from the water.*

grand adjective

Something that is **grand** seems very important.
*The King and Queen looked very **grand**.*

> 1) **dignified** 2) **impressive** 3) **glorious** 4) **majestic**

1) *Ben's dad looked **dignified** in his new suit.*
2) *The visitors thought the palace was very **impressive**.*
3) *The old people had a **glorious** day out in the country.*
4) *The opera singer wore very **majestic** clothes.*

Opposites: **humble, modest**

great adjective

If something is **great**, it is large in size or in number.
*There was a **great** steeple on top of the church.*

> 1) **big** 2) **immense** 3) **enormous** 4) **vast**

1) *The **big** cruise ship sailed into the harbor.*
2) *The researcher had an **immense** knowledge of his subject.*
3) *The young vet had an **enormous** love of animals.*
4) *A **vast** crowd gathered to see the parade.*

Opposites: **little, small, tiny**

greedy adjective

If you are **greedy**, you eat more than your fair share.
*The **greedy** boy ate the whole cake.*

> 1) **gluttonous** 2) **voracious** 3) **selfish**

1) *The **gluttonous** pig never stopped eating.*
2) *The **voracious** queen wanted more food than anyone else.*
3) *The **selfish** boy would not share his candy with his sister.*

group adjective

A **group** is a collection of people, animals, or things.
*A small **group** of singers is called a choir.*

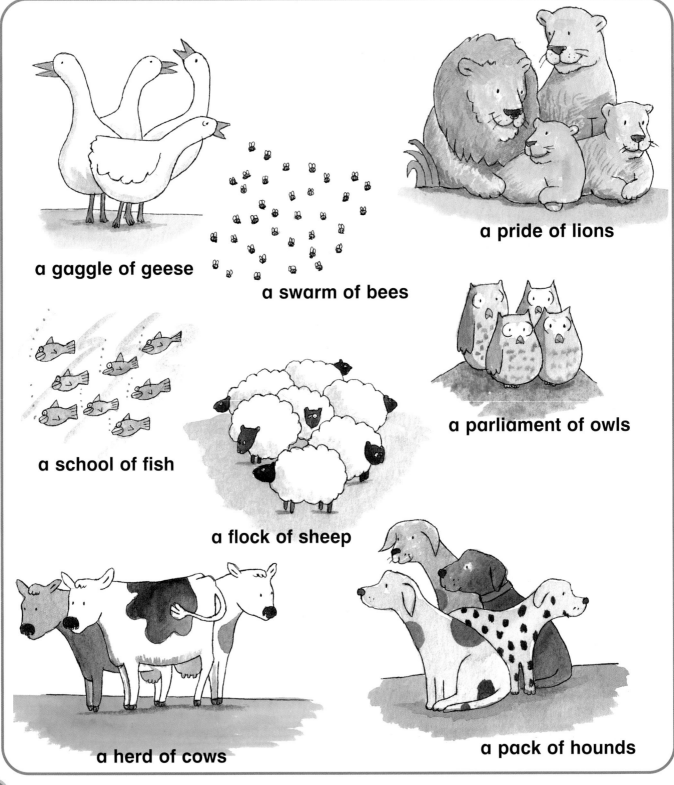

a gaggle of geese

a swarm of bees

a pride of lions

a school of fish

a flock of sheep

a parliament of owls

a herd of cows

a pack of hounds

grow verb

When something **grows** it gets bigger.
The sunflowers started to grow above the wall.

> 1) **develop** 2) **increase** 3) **swell**

1) *Small seeds develop into leafy plants.*
2) *The fund for the new school quickly increased.*
3) *The balloon swelled as I blew into it.*

Opposite: **shrink**

guess verb

If you **guess** something, you think it is right, but you are not sure.
The burglar guessed where the key was hidden.

> 1) **think** 2) **estimate** 3) **suspect**

1) *I think I might get a new surfboard for my birthday.*
2) *The carpenter estimated that it would take a week to make the cabinet.*
3) *The police officer suspected that the mystery thief was a man.*

guide verb

If you **guide** someone, you show that person how to do or find something.
The local people guided the explorers through the jungle.

> 1) **direct** 2) **lead** 3) **accompany** 4) **usher**

1) *The police officer directed the traffic.*
2) *The firefighter led the patients out of the burning hospital.*
3) *My older sister accompanied us to the recreation center.*
4) *The officials ushered the athletes into the sports village.*

handsome adjective

A **handsome** person is good looking.
*The **handsome** prince had married a beautiful princess.*

> 1) **attractive** 2) **fine** 3) **good-looking**

1) *The bride and groom made an **attractive** couple.*
2) *The model had a very **fine** face.*
3) *Mrs. Allen was proud of her **good-looking** son.*

Opposite: **ugly**

happen verb

If something **happens**, it occurs or takes place.
*Accidents can **happen** if you take risks.*

> 1) **take place** 2) **occur** 3) **come about** 4) **arise**

1) *Jamie's party **took place** at the bowling alley.*
2) *Your birthday **occurs** on the same date each year.*
3) *Flooding may **come about** after a heavy storm.*
4) *An argument **arose** between the two baseball teams.*

happy adjective

If you are **happy**, you feel pleased.
*Sarah had a very **happy** eighth birthday.*

> 1) **blissful** 2) **contented** 3) **delighted** 4) **thrilled**

1) *The children had a **blissful** vacation at the lake.*
2) *Mark was a very **contented** baby.*
3) *I was **delighted** to get an invitation to
   the opening of the new art gallery.*
4) *Josh was **thrilled** to get a part in the
   school play.*

Opposites: **sad, unhappy**

hard adjective

If something is **hard**, it is very difficult.
*The students did not like the **hard** math test.*

1) **tough** 2) **difficult** 3) **demanding**

1) *It was **tough** work planting the new trees.*
2) *It was **difficult** to find a cure for the disease.*
3) *The teacher gave us some **demanding** homework.*

Opposite: **easy**

hard adjective

A **hard** object is firm and solid.
*The bridge was made of **hard** concrete.*

1) **rigid** 2) **firm** 3) **unyielding**

1) *The fragile statue was packed in a **rigid** container.*
2) *You have to put a bathroom scale on a **firm** surface.*
3) *It was impossible to push open the **unyielding** door.*

Opposite: **soft**

harm verb

To **harm** means to hurt someone or something.
*Alex was careful not to **harm** the butterfly.*

1) **damage** 2) **hurt** 3) **injure** 4) **ruin**

1) *Very strong winds may **damage** buildings.*
2) *When the horse fell over it **hurt** its leg.*
3) *It is cruel to **injure** animals.*
4) *Spilling milk onto a table will **ruin** the wood.*

Opposites: **benefit, help**

Hh hat

hat noun

A **hat** is an item of clothing that you wear on your head.
*I tried on an interesting **hat** in the store.*

ski cap

bonnet

baseball cap

deerstalker

panama

top hat

sunhat

hate adjective

If you **hate** something, you do not like it at all.
*We **hate** eating Brussels sprouts.*

1) **despise** 2) **detest** 3) **dislike** 4) **loathe**

1) *We all **despise** bullies at school.*
2) *Some people **detest** spiders.*
3) *I **dislike** doing my homework.*
4) *Kelly **loathes** straightening her bedroom.*

Opposites: **like, love**

kneel verb

To **kneel** is to get down on your knees.
*The prince **kneeled** and asked the princess to marry him.*

> 1) **bend** 2) **bow down** 3) **stoop**

1) *She had to **bend** down to talk to the child.*
2) *The priests **bowed down** in front of the altar.*
3) *Grandpa **stooped** to smell the flowers.*

knock verb

To **knock** means to hit or bang.
*Jack reached up to **knock** on the front door.*

> 1) **hit** 2) **rap** 3) **tap** 4) **bang**

1) *The batter **hit** the ball past third base.*
2) *The librarian sometimes has to **rap** on the desk to get our attention.*
3) *The carpenter **tapped** the nail with a hammer.*
4) *Shirley **banged** on the window until we let her in.*

knot verb

If you **knot** something, you tie together two pieces of rope or string.
*The sailor **knotted** the ropes to attach the sails.*

> 1) **tie** 2) **loop** 3) **bind** 4) **secure**

1) *"I can **tie** my shoelaces now!" said Carly.*
2) *Mom **looped** the string around both packages.*
3) *The nurse had to **bind** the cut on my hand with a bandage.*
4) *Ben **secured** his bike to the fence with a bike chain.*

Opposites: **unfasten, untie**

know verb

If you **know** about something, you understand it.
*Dad and Patrick **know** how to put up a tent.*

1) **realize** 2) **understand** 3) **see** 4) **be sure of**

1) *The actress didn't **realize** how late she was.*
2) *The children **understood** why their mom was so annoyed with them.*
3) *She could **see** why her math homework was wrong.*
4) *The angry customer **was sure of** his facts.*

know verb

If you **know** someone, you recognize that person.
*Tom **knew** all the people at his birthday party.*

1) **identify** 2) **recognize** 3) **remember**

1) *The woman told the police that she could **identify** the thief.*
2) *Although the sisters had not met for 20 years, they **recognized** each other instantly.*
3) *Jason **remembered** all his friends from his old club.*

knowledge noun

If you have **knowledge** about something, you know facts about it.
*All the contestants had good general **knowledge**.*

1) **experience** 2) **understanding** 3) **grasp**

1) *The mountaineer had a wealth of **experience**.*
2) *The researcher's **understanding** of the disease was excellent.*
3) *The new recruits wanted to **grasp** how to sail a boat.*

Opposite: **ignorance**

land noun

Land is the solid earth under your feet.
The rich man owned lots of land.

> 1) **ground** 2) **soil** 3) **earth**

1) *The **ground** was too hard to dig.*
2) *The farmer plows the **soil** with his new tractor.*
3) *Crops grow well in good **earth**.*

land verb

To **land** means to stop traveling and come to rest on land or water.
*The helicopter **landed** on the hotel roof.*

> 1) **touch down** 2) **arrive** 3) **alight**

1) *The plane **touched down** on the runway.*
2) *The boat **arrived** at a desert island.*
3) *A wasp **alighted** on the soldier's nose.*

Opposite: **take off**

large adjective

If something is **large** it is very big.
*My aunt received a **large** package in the mail.*

> 1) **big** 2) **massive** 3) **colossal** 4) **enormous**

1) *A toucan has a **big**, colorful beak.*
2) *The weightlifter has **massive** shoulders.*
3) *We looked up at the **colossal** building.*
4) *The giant had a pair of **enormous** feet!*

Opposites: **little, small, tiny**

last adjective

If something is **last**, it is the final one.
The letter z is the last letter of the alphabet.

> 1) **closing** 2) **final** 3) **concluding**

1) *A goal was scored in the **closing** minute of the game.*
2) *The penalty shoot-out was the **final** chance to win the match.*
3) *The **concluding** episode of the film was very exciting.*

Opposites: **first, initial, opening**

last verb

If something **lasts**, it stays in place.
*A stone house is built to **last**.*

> 1) **endure** 2) **continue** 3) **persist**

1) *Shakespeare's work has **endured** long after his death.*
2) *Isabel wanted the music to **continue** forever.*
3) *The tropical rain **persisted** for three days.*

late adjective

If you are **late**, you arrive after the agreed time.
*Jenny was **late** for swimming practice.*

> 1) **behind** 2) **delayed** 3) **overdue** 4) **belated**

1) *I am **behind** with my school project.*
2) *The **delayed** train arrived two hours later.*
3) *My books are **overdue** at the library.*
4) *I received a **belated** Christmas present in January.*

Opposites: **early, on time**

laugh verb

When you **laugh**, you make a happy sound because something is funny.
People always laugh at my uncle's jokes.

> 1) **chuckle** 2) **giggle** 3) **guffaw** 4) **chortle**

1) *We started to **chuckle** when we saw the little pink monster on TV.*
2) *I could not stop **giggling** when I heard the funny story.*
3) *The ridiculous story made us **guffaw**.*
4) *Everyone **chortled** at the funny play.*

Opposites: **cry, sob, weep**

layer noun

A **layer** is something flat that sits above or below a surface.
The ground was covered with a layer of snow.

> 1) **coating** 2) **film** 3) **sheet**

1) *The cake had a **coating** of white icing.*
2) *There was a **film** of dust over the furniture.*
3) *The car skidded on a **sheet** of ice.*

lazy adjective

If you are **lazy**, you do not want to do any work.
Jack was a lazy boy who stayed in bed all day.

> 1) **idle** 2) **slothful** 3) **careless** 4) **indolent**

1) *Sarah was **idle** and did not go outside to play.*
3) *The **slothful** boy never straightened his bedroom.*
4) *The store's employees had a very **careless** way of working.*
1) *The **indolent** waitress was always sitting down.*

Opposites: **active, busy, energetic**

Ll lead

lead verb

To **lead** means to show someone the way.
*The guide has to **lead** the tourists past the ruins.*

> 1) **guide** 2) **conduct** 3) **escort** 4) **usher**

1) *She **guided** the blind man across the street.*
2) *The waiter **conducted** us to our table.*
3) *Charlotte **escorted** her parents to their seats.*
4) *The manager **ushered** us into the dining room.*

Opposite: **follow**

leave verb

When you **leave**, you go away.
*When I **leave** home I'm going to take my cat with me.*

> 1) **go** 2) **depart** 3) **make tracks** 4) **set out**

1) *We have to **go** to our tent before it gets dark.*
2) *We planned to **depart** at six o'clock.*
3) *Toward the end of the party the guests began to **make tracks** for home.*
4) *I **set out** for school right after breakfast.*

Opposites: **arrive, come**

lie verb

To **lie** means to rest in a flat position.
*Mom went to **lie** down after lunch.*

> 1) **be recumbent** 2) **recline** 3) **lounge**

1) *The princess **was recumbent** on a velvet couch.*
2) *Jasmine **reclined** on her bed.*
3) *My brother likes to **lounge** on the sofa.*

Opposite: **stand**

light adjective

If something is **light** it does not weigh very much and is easy to carry.
*The small bag was **light** enough to carry onto the plane.*

> 1) **flimsy** 2) **lightweight** 3) **slight**

1) *She wore a **flimsy** dress because it was such a hot day.*
2) *A feather is **lightweight** when compared to a bone.*
3) *My younger cousin is small and **slight**.*

Opposite: **heavy**

light noun

A **light** is an object that shines and makes the area around it bright.
*You turn on the **light** when you walk into a dark hall.*

flashlight

headlight

candle

lightbulb

table lamp

lantern

streetlight

like verb

If you **like** something, you are pleased with it.
*"I **like** this sweater best," said Lauren.*

> 1) **admire** 2) **enjoy** 3) **be fond of**

1) *The jeweler **admired** the new silver brooch.*
2) *Grandma **enjoys** baking cakes.*
3) *Anna **is fond of** her next-door neighbor.*

Opposites: **dislike, hate**

like adjective

If one thing is **like** another, it is the same or similar.
*Mom's new car was **like** her old one.*

> 1) **identical to** 2) **comparable to** 3) **similar to**

1) *Lisa's outfit was **identical to** her twin sister's.*
2) *The professor's discoveries are **comparable to** mine.*
3) *My brother looks **similar to** me.*

Opposites: **unlike, dissimilar to**

litter noun

Litter is garbage that people throw on the ground.
*There was **litter** all over our street.*

> 1) **trash** 2) **garbage** 3) **waste** 4) **debris**

1) *You should always throw your **trash** in the wastebasket.*
2) *Our **garbage** is collected every Thursday.*
3) *The **waste** from the steel factory goes into the local river.*
4) ***Debris** from the sunken ship floated to the surface.*

little adjective

If something is **little** it is small or tiny.
*The toddler was too **little** to go on the Big Dipper.*

> 1) **small** 2) **miniature** 3) **minute** 4) **tiny**

1) *We planted a **small** tree in the garden.*
2) *My grandma collects **miniature** teapots.*
3) *The **minute** beetle crept through the keyhole.*
4) *The baby wore **tiny** mittens on her hands.*

Opposites: **big, large**

lonely adjective

If you are **lonely** you feel sad because you are alone.
*Jamal was **lonely** when all his friends went home.*

> 1) **friendless** 2) **alone** 3) **solitary** 4) **forsaken**

1) *The **friendless** boy sat at a desk by himself.*
2) *The old lady lived **alone** in a big house.*
3) *The artist was a **solitary** man.*
4) *The puppy felt **forsaken** when its owner went away.*

long adjective

If something is **long** it lasts for more time than usual.
*It was a **long** trip to the seashore.*

> 1) **endless** 2) **lengthy** 3) **extended**

1) *The **endless** lecture was very boring.*
2) *The teacher gave a **lengthy** explanation about the Solar System.*
3) *I took an **extended** vacation in Australia.*

Opposite: **short**

Beach
25 miles

long for verb

To **long for** something means to wish for it strongly.
*The children **longed for** their math class to end.*

> 1) **yearn** 2) **crave** 3) **hunger** 4) **desire**

1) *The immigrant **yearned** to go back home.*
2) *He **craved** all the cakes and pastries he saw.*
3) *They **hungered** for some more interesting books.*
4) *The astronauts **desired** to return to Earth.*

look verb

To **look** means to turn your eyes toward
someone or something.
*Jack went to **look** at the new house.*

> 1) **examine** 2) **gaze** 3) **stare** 4) **watch**

1) *The doctor had to **examine** the wound.*
2) *The artist **gazed** at the beautiful painting.*
3) *Dan knew it was rude to **stare** at people.*
4) *I **watched** the bird through my binoculars.*

lose verb

If you **lose** something, you cannot find it.
*"Put the money in your purse so you don't **lose** it!" said Mom.*

> 1) **misplace** 2) **mislay** 3) **drop**

1) *Jenny **misplaced** her textbook and had to buy a new one.*
2) *Dad **mislays** his car keys all the time.*
3) *The baby has **dropped** her doll somewhere in the house.*

Opposite: **find**

loud adjective

If something is **loud**, it is very noisy.
*The plate fell to the floor with a **loud** crash.*

> 1) **blaring** 2) **deafening** 3) **noisy** 4) **thunderous**

1) The **blaring** music disturbed everyone.
2) A jackhammer makes a **deafening** noise.
3) The **noisy** mob stormed through the streets.
4) Uncle Jed has a **thunderous** voice.

Opposites: **low, quiet, soft**

love verb

If you **love** someone or something, that person or thing
means a lot to you.
*Daniel **loves** his parents very much.*

> 1) **adore** 2) **worship** 3) **dote on**

1) I **adore** my new kitten.
2) The small boy **worships** his older brother.
3) Professor Williams **doted on** his students.

Opposite: **hate**

lovely adjective

If something is **lovely**, it is delightful or pretty.
*The bride is wearing a **lovely** silk dress.*

> 1) **attractive** 2) **beautiful** 3) **exquisite**

1) The model wore an **attractive** hat.
2) **Beautiful** flowers grow in the garden.
3) My sister has some **exquisite** jewelry.

Opposites: **hideous, ugly**

machine noun

A **machine** is a piece of equipment with parts that work together to do a special job.
*A washing **machine** cleans clothes.*

1) **device** 2) **apparatus** 3) **tool**

1) *Professor Sparks invented a **device** for cleaning his house.*
2) *There was a lot of **apparatus** in the laboratory.*
3) *Dad has a special **tool** for cleaning out the gutters.*

mad adjective

If you are **mad**, you are very angry.
*The **mad** bull charged at the farmer.*

1) **furious** 2) **irate** 3) **raging** 4) **seething**

1) *The athlete was **furious** when he lost the race.*
2) *Our dog was **irate** when the cat ate his food.*
3) *The **raging** pirate jumped off his ship into the ocean.*
4) *The grumpy old man was **seething** with anger.*

magic noun

Magic is the use of spells to do clever things.
*The wizard used **magic** to get his dishes washed.*

1) **sorcery** 2) **witchcraft** 3) **wizardry**

1) *The puppet was brought to life by **sorcery**.*
2) *Polly wanted to learn about **witchcraft**.*
3) *"My **wizardry** will turn you into a frog," cackled the wizard.*

main adjective

Main means the most important.
*I played the **main** character in the school play.*

> 1) **chief** 2) **principal** 3) **prime** 4) **head**

1) *"The **chief** problem is the leaking roof," said the builder.*
2) *The **principal** ballerina is very tall.*
3) *Roger the Robber is our **prime** suspect.*
4) *The **head** officer on board a ship is called a captain.*

Opposite: **minor**

make verb

To **make** means to force a person or an object to do something.
*"Don't **make** me go to the haunted house!" squealed Rosie.*

> 1) **compel** 2) **force** 3) **oblige**

1) *The rain **compelled** me to put up my umbrella.*
2) *Sam's brother **forced** him to tell lies.*
3) *"Don't **oblige** me to separate you," warned the teacher.*

make verb

When you **make** something, you build it or put it together.
*Mom asked Sarah to **make** dinner.*

> 1) **create** 2) **build** 3) **produce**

1) *It is fun to **create** colorful pots with clay.*
2) *"I want to **build** a sand castle," said Scott.*
3) *The big factory **produces** cars.*

Opposite: **destroy**

many   adjective

Many means a large number of something.
*Tim had **many** friends at his new school.*

> 1) **abundant** 2) **countless** 3) **numerous** 4) **a lot of**

1) *"We have an **abundant** corn crop this year,"
   said the farmer.*
2) *Joe made **countless** trips to the candy store.*
3) *The class read **numerous** books about space.*
4) *There were **a lot of** skateboards for sale.*

Opposite: **few**

march   verb

To **march** is to walk with quick steps like a soldier.
*The battalion of soldiers **marched** across the parade ground.*

> 1) **stride** 2) **parade** 3) **file** 4) **troop**

1) *After a while the walkers at the front began to **stride** out.*
2) *The new cadets will **parade** in front of their general.*
3) *The prisoners **filed** out of their cells.*
4) *When they heard the fire alarm, the audience **trooped** out of the theater.*

mark   noun

A **mark** is a dirty spot.
*I scrubbed the oily **marks** off my jeans.*

> 1) **stain** 2) **smudge** 3) **spot** 4) **smear**

1) *The **stain** would not come out of her evening gown.*
2) *The artist made a **smudge** on his drawing.*
3) *I have a **spot** on my silk tie.*
4) *We found a large **smear** on the window.*

match noun

A **match** is an event in which two people, or two teams, play against each other.
*The whole family watched the **match** on TV.*

> 1) **competition** 2) **contest** 3) **game**

1) *We cheered when our team won the **competition**.*
2) *She challenged me to a jumprope **contest**.*
3) *The baseball **game** lasted for hours.*

matter noun

A **matter** is a subject or business that you need to think about or do.
*"We should talk about this **matter**," said the doctor.*

> 1) **issue** 2) **topic** 3) **subject**

1) *The most important **issue** was the increase in nuclear power.*
2) *Our school held a debate on the **topic** of recycling.*
3) *Martin is passionate about the **subject** of politics.*

meal noun

A **meal** is the food that you sit down to eat at different times of the day.
*"Breakfast is my favorite **meal** of the day," said Mom.*

> 1) **feast** 2) **snack** 3) **banquet**

1) *A delicious **feast** was spread out on the blanket.*
2) *We had a quick **snack** on our way to the airport.*
3) *The king held a **banquet** for his guests.*

mean adjective

If you are **mean**, you are unkind to others.
*Mom told me not to be **mean** to my little sister.*

> 1) **nasty** 2) **unfriendly** 3) **cruel** 4) **selfish**

1) *A bully at school was really **nasty** to me today.*
2) *Stay away from that dog—it looks **unfriendly**.*
3) *We should never be **cruel** to animals.*
4) *Thomas was **selfish** and wouldn't share his toys.*

Opposites: **kind, friendly, generous**

mean verb

What someone or something **means** is what that person
or thing is trying to tell you.
*"I don't understand what you **mean**," said the student.*

> 1) **imply** 2) **indicate** 3) **signify**

1) *His smile **implied** that he was joking.*
2) *A red light **indicates** that you cannot cross the street.*
3) *Dark clouds **signify** that it is going to rain.*

meet verb

To **meet** is to come together.
*"Let's **meet** at the movie," suggested Annie.*

> 1) **assemble** 2) **gather** 3) **congregate**

1) *The crowd **assembled** outside the town hall.*
2) *We **gather** in the playground every morning.*
3) *Maisy's friends **congregated** in front of her house.*

melt verb

To **melt** is to change to a liquid when heated.
When the sun came out, the snowman began to melt.

> 1) **dissolve** 2) **unfreeze** 3) **thaw**

1) *When you add sugar to tea it dissolves.*
2) *I unfreeze my dinner in the microwave.*
3) *Ice thaws when the sun shines.*

Opposites: **freeze, harden**

mend verb

To **mend** something means to repair it.
Matthew tried to mend his punctured tire.

> 1) **repair** 2) **darn** 3) **fix**

1) *The builders repaired the hole in the roof.*
2) *Aunt Ethel always darns her husband's socks.*
3) *"I've fixed the motorcycle!" grinned the new mechanic.*

Opposite: **break**

mess noun

A **mess** is an untidy confusion of things.
"Clean up this mess!" yelled Mom.

> 1) **chaos** 2) **shambles** 3) **jumble** 4) **clutter**

1) *The room was chaos after the party.*
2) *"My desk is a shambles," cried May.*
3) *We helped sort out the jumble
   of clothes.*
4) *The kitchen table was buried under
   the clutter.*

Opposites: **order, tidiness**

metal noun

A **metal** is a hard material that can be used to make many things.
Our knives and forks are made of **metal.**

tray

scissors

fence

necklace

candlestick

ring

scooter

fork

middle noun

The **middle** is the point that is halfway between two other points.
White lines are painted down the **middle** *of the road.*

1) **center** 2) **core** 3) **heart**

1) *I never eat the pits at the* **center** *of my apple.*
2) *It is very hot at the Earth's* **core.**
3) *The statue stands in the* **heart** *of our city.*

mild adjective

If something is **mild**, it is gentle.
*There was a **mild** breeze as we sailed out to sea.*

1) **gentle** 2) **serene** 3) **pleasant**

1) *Annabelle is a very **gentle** person.*
2) *Our horse has a **serene** temperament.*
3) *"We had **pleasant** weather on our vacation,"
   smiled George.*

mind noun

Your **mind** is the part of you that lets you think, feel, remember, and understand.
*Jake's clever **mind** soon figured out the puzzle.*

1) **brain** 2) **intellect** 3) **intelligence**

1) *My **brain** was tired after a day of studying!*
2) *"Use your **intellect** to answer the question," said Mr. Mason.*
3) *Everyone admired the smart child's sharp **intelligence**.*

miss verb

If you **miss** someone, you are sad because that person
is no longer with you.
*Carl **missed** the mountains when he went to live in the city.*

1) **pine** 2) **long for** 3) **want**

1) *The dog **pined** for its owners when they went away.*
2) *When I moved school I **longed for** my old friends.*
3) *Mark was homesick and **wanted** his mom.*

miss verb

If you **miss**, you fail to find or hit a target.
*We all groaned when the goalkeeper **missed** the ball.*

> 1) **avoid** 2) **evade** 3) **dodge**

1) *We left early to **avoid** the rush hour.*
2) *The crafty jewel thief **evaded** the police.*
3) *"No one is going to **dodge** Field Day!"
   shouted the sports teacher.*

Opposites: **find, hit**

mistake noun

A **mistake** is something that you do wrong, or the wrong thing.
*I made lots of **mistakes** in my spelling test.*

> 1) **blunder** 2) **error** 3) **oversight**

1) *The clumsy man apologized for his **blunder**.*
2) *"I made an **error** when I trusted you," snapped the supervisor.*
3) *Because of an **oversight** we missed the last train.*

mix verb

To **mix** means to put together.
*Mom had to **mix** the ingredients for my birthday cake.*

> 1) **blend** 2) **combine** 3) **mingle** 4) **merge**

1) *The painter **blended** the colors carefully.*
2) *You **combine** eggs with milk to make an omelet.*
3) *The funny clown **mingled** with the audience.*
4) *All the classes **merged** for a dancing lesson.*

Opposite: **separate**

moan noun

A **moan** is an unhappy sound that shows you are in pain or in trouble.
*The patient gave a **moan** as the doctor felt his stomach.*

> 1) **groan** 2) **wail** 3) **sob** 4) **whine**

1) *We heard a **groan** coming from the closet.*
2) *I let out a **wail** when I saw the ghost!*
3) *My sister's loud **sob** woke me up.*
4) *The dog's **whine** was a horrible noise.*

modern adjective

If something is **modern** it is up to date.
*My dad hates **modern** music.*

> 1) **latest** 2) **contemporary** 3) **fashionable** 4) **current**

1) *"I only wear the **latest** clothes," said the model.*
2) *The **contemporary** furniture looked odd in the old house.*
3) *My aunt wears very **fashionable** shoes.*
4) *I like to read books by **current** writers.*

Opposites: **dated, old-fashioned**

money noun

Money is the bills and coins you use to buy things.
*I earn extra **money** by delivering newspapers.*

> 1) **cash** 2) **change** 3) **funds** 4) **riches**

1) *Dad gave me some **cash** to buy new sneakers.*
2) *"Have you got any **change** for the soda machine?" Kathy asked.*
3) *He saved up his **funds** to buy a new car.*
4) *All the king's **riches** couldn't buy him what he wanted.*

monster noun

A **monster** is an imaginary beast.
I read about **monsters**
in fairy tales.

giant

dragon

beast

werewolf

goblin

ogre

troll

move verb

To **move** is to change the place or position of something.
*"**Move** your feet closer together!" cried the gym coach.*

1) **carry** 2) **push** 3) **transfer**

1) *The movers **carry** the sofa down the stairs.*
2) *"**Push** those boxes out of the way!" said Dad.*
3) *I **transferred** the heavy bag to my other hand.*

mumble verb

To **mumble** is to speak unclearly in a quiet voice.
*"Speak up! I can't hear you when you **mumble**," said Grandpa.*

1) **murmur** 2) **mutter** 3) **whisper**

1) *She heard some people **murmur** behind her in the elevator.*
2) *David **muttered** angrily to himself when he tripped on his shoelaces.*
3) *"Help me!" **whispered** the injured soldier.*

mystery noun

A **mystery** is something puzzling that you cannot explain.
*The detective was working on a strange **mystery**.*

1) **puzzle** 2) **riddle** 3) **enigma**

1) *A smart girl solved the **puzzle** of Grace's missing glasses.*
2) *"I love a good **riddle**," chuckled my uncle.*
3) *Where the new science teacher had come from was an **enigma**.*

narrow adjective

If something is **narrow**, it is small in width.
*The man walked down the **narrow** street.*

> 1) **thin** 2) **slender** 3) **slim**

1) *Canal boats are long and **thin**.*
2) *The model had a **slender** waist.*
3) *We squeezed through the **slim** space in the fence.*

Opposites: **broad, wide**

nasty adjective

To be **nasty** means to be very unpleasant.
*The **nasty** girl hit her little brother.*

> 1) **spiteful** 2) **unkind** 3) **vile** 4) **vicious**

1) *Richard is a **spiteful** boy.*
2) *"Don't be so **unkind**," said Archie.*
3) *My **vile** cousin always pulls my hair.*
4) *Martha had a **vicious** temper.*

Opposite: **nice**

naughty adjective

To be **naughty** means to behave badly.
*The **naughty** twins tired out their babysitter.*

> 1) **disobedient** 2) **bad** 3) **impish**

1) *Ted was **disobedient** and broke the rules.*
2) *"**Bad** dog!" said Dad when he saw the mess.*
3) *The **impish** child was always in trouble.*

Opposites: **good, polite, well-behaved**

near adjective

Near means close to something.
*"I love living **near** the ocean," said the old sailor.*

> 1) **adjacent** 2) **beside** 3) **close** 4) **neighboring**

1) *The two houses had **adjacent** front doors.*
2) *Our house is **beside** a stream.*
3) *Jenny lived **close** to her best friend.*
4) *Henry threw trash in the **neighboring** yard.*

Opposites: **distant, far**

neat adjective

To be **neat** means to be tidy.
*Pat has very **neat** handwriting.*

> 1) **tidy** 2) **orderly** 3) **trim**

1) *David liked to keep his room **tidy**.*
2) *"It is important to be **orderly**,"*
   said the captain.
3) *Laura looked wonderful in her **trim** suit.*

Opposite: **messy, untidy**

need verb

To **need** means to want something urgently.
*"I **need** more fruit," said Mom.*

> 1) **crave** 2) **require** 3) **want**

1) *"I **crave** some chocolate," sighed Helen.*
2) *To make a greeting card you **require** paper, a pencil,*
   and some paints.
3) *Ted and Ravi **want** spaghetti for dinner.*

nervous adjective

To be **nervous** is to be easily scared or worried.
*Sarah felt **nervous** when she saw the big dog.*

1) **anxious** 2) **uneasy** 3) **timid** 4) **edgy**

1) *Alice was **anxious** about her science test.*
2) *Grandma was **uneasy** about flying in a plane.*
3) *Mice are **timid** creatures.*
4) *I got **edgy** when I heard the door creak open.*

Opposites: **calm, relaxed**

new adjective

If something is **new** it has just been made, thought, or bought.
*Aunt Jesse bought a **new** hat for Easter.*

1) **fresh** 2) **original** 3) **novel**

1) *The teacher asked for some **fresh** ideas.*
2) *We saw an **original** play at the new theater.*
3) *Norman has a **novel** diet plan.*

Opposite: **old**

next adjective

The **next** is the one that comes right after.
*We waited to catch the **next** bus.*

1) **subsequent** 2) **following** 3) **later**

1) *"I'll take the **subsequent** train," said Jack.*
2) *The circus arrived the **following** day.*
3) *They went to the **later** showing at the movies.*

Opposite: **previous**

nice adjective

Something that is **nice** is pleasing.
*Daisy had a **nice**, relaxing afternoon.*

> 1) **pleasant** 2) **agreeable** 3) **charming**

1) *The house had a **pleasant** garden.*
2) *Lucy's new boyfriend was very **agreeable**.*
3) *The **charming** boy shook hands with the visitor.*

Opposites: **nasty, horrid, unpleasant**

noisy adjective

If something is **noisy** it is too loud.
*The **noisy** dog wouldn't stop barking.*

> 1) **deafening** 2) **loud** 3) **strident** 4) **piercing**

1) *The music at the disco was **deafening**.*
2) *The jet's engines made a **loud** noise as the plane took off.*
3) *"You've got a very **strident** voice," said the nurse.*
4) *Shelley let out a **piercing** scream.*

Opposites: **quiet**

nonsense noun

Words, actions, or ideas that are **nonsense** are silly or have no meaning.
*Mr. Lewin said that Robert's story was a lot of **nonsense**.*

> 1) **gibberish** 2) **drivel** 3) **silliness**

1) *The madman was talking **gibberish**.*
2) *"You're talking **drivel**," snapped the captain.*
3) *"Stop this **silliness**," ordered our math teacher.*

Opposite: **sense**

normal adjective

If something is **normal**, it is usual and what you would expect.
*The school bus left at the **normal** time.*

> 1) **usual** 2) **ordinary** 3) **regular** 4) **average**

1) *The **usual** driver was taking a sick day.*
2) *The magician held up an **ordinary** cap.*
3) *I bought a **regular**-size soda.*
4) *"He's an **average** student," said the music teacher.*

Opposites: **strange, abnormal**

nosy adjective

To be **nosy** is to snoop or interfere.
***Nosy** Norma was always peeking through keyholes.*

> 1) **inquisitive** 2) **prying** 3) **snooping**

1) *"Don't be so **inquisitive**," grinned Dad.*
2) *I hid my designs away from **prying** eyes.*
3) *The **snooping** detective found all the clues
   he needed.*

Opposite: **uninterested**

nothing noun

Nothing is the absence of something.
*Donald had **nothing** to do.*

> 1) **emptiness** 2) **zero** 3) **blank**

1) *There was **emptiness** where my bike should have been.*
2) *The temperature fell to **zero** overnight.*
3) *I tried to remember her name, but my mind was a **blank**.*

Opposite: **something**

notice noun

A **notice** is a sign that gives information.
*The principal pinned a **notice** on the bulletin board.*

> 1) **advertisement** 2) **sign** 3) **poster**

1) *We put an **advertisement** in the newspaper.*
2) *The **sign** said "Closed For Repairs."*
3) *The **poster** says that the circus is coming next week.*

notice verb

To **notice** is to see or observe.
*Eileen **noticed** that her garden was flooded.*

> 1) **spot** 2) **observe** 3) **detect**

1) *"Did you **spot** me on TV?" asked William.*
2) *Oliver **observed** a rare bird in the garden.*
3) *We all **detected** a strange smell.*

Opposite: **miss**

nuisance noun

A **nuisance** is something or someone that is annoying.
*My little sister is a terrible **nuisance**.*

> 1) **pain** 2) **pest** 3) **irritation**

1) *It was a **pain** to have to go out in the rain.*
2) *"Don't be such a **pest**!" yelled my brother.*
3) *The sound of drilling in the street is
   a big **irritation**.*

obedient adjective

If you are **obedient**, you do as you are told.
*The **obedient** dog came to his owner when she called.*

> 1) **dutiful** 2) **submissive** 3) **respectful**

1) *The **dutiful** daughter looked after her parents.*
2) *Jeff is a **submissive** person.*
3) *The **respectful** servant bowed to the king.*

Opposites: **disobedient, rebellious**

object noun

The **object** is the main purpose or target.
*The **object** of a soccer game is to score lots of goals.*

> 1) **aim** 2) **goal** 3) **purpose**

1) *Jim's **aim** in life was to become very rich!*
2) *Mom's **goal** was to clean the whole yard.*
3) *The **purpose** of going to the market was to buy some fruit.*

object noun

An **object** is a thing you can touch and see.
*We had to guess what the **object** was with our eyes closed.*

> 1) **article** 2) **thing** 3) **item**

1) *Maureen held the strange **article** in her hand.*
2) *The new computer was a tiny **thing**.*
3) *There were five **items** in my purse.*

odd adjective

If something is **odd**, it is different or unusual.
*Dad had an **odd** expression on his face.*

> 1) **weird** 2) **bizarre** 3) **peculiar** 4) **strange**

1) *Andrea dyed her hair a **weird** color.*
2) *"What a **bizarre** boat!" exclaimed the sailor.*
3) *Jane's **peculiar** accent was hard to understand.*
4) *A **strange** noise came from the closet.*

Opposite: **normal**

often adverb

Often means frequently.
*Jason **often** visited the zoo.*

> 1) **frequently** 2) **much** 3) **repeatedly**

1) *The buses to town run **frequently**.*
2) *Shakespeare is a **much**-quoted writer.*
3) *Dave recited the poem **repeatedly**.*

Opposites: **rarely, seldom**

old adjective

If something is **old**, it has existed for a long time.
*Mom wore **old** jeans for gardening.*

> 1) **aged** 2) **ancient** 3) **elderly**

1) *The **aged** wizard had a long white beard.*
2) *There is an **ancient** table in the living room.*
3) *My grandma is an **elderly** lady.*

Opposites: **new, young**

Oo old

old adjective

If something is **old**, it is the one that came before.
*Our **old** house had five bedrooms.*

> 1) **earlier** 2) **former** 3) **previous**

1) *"This camera is better than the **earlier** model,"
   grinned Ron.*
2) *Andy's **former** job was driving steamrollers.*
3) *My **previous** teacher was very kind.*

Opposites: **current, present**

once adverb

Once means at one time in the past.
*I **once** ran a mile in five minutes.*

> 1) **formerly** 2) **previously** 3) **at one time**

1) *Mrs. Evans was **formerly** a beauty queen.*
2) *Our house was **previously** a monastery.*
3) ***At one time**, dinosaurs roamed the Earth.*

only adjective

If something is **only** it is a single one.
*Dan was an **only** child.*

> 1) **lone** 2) **sole** 3) **solitary**

1) *She was the **lone** girl in the scout group.*
2) *"Football is my **sole** interest," said Gary.*
3) *The waiter was the **solitary** witness to the crime.*

only adverb

Only means nothing more than.
*There were **only** three chips left in the bag.*

> 1) **just** 2) **merely** 3) **totally**

1) *We had **just** 30 seconds to answer the question.*
2) *"You're **merely** a child," said the nasty man.*
3) *"That story is **totally** made up," said the reporter.*

open verb

To **open** means to move or change from a closed position.
*Many stores **open** at nine o'clock in the morning.*

> 1) **unwrap** 2) **unfasten** 3) **uncork**

1) *Maya quickly **unwrapped** her presents.*
2) *The burglar **unfastened** the window.*
3) *Uncle Bert said he would **uncork** the
   bottle of wine.*

Opposites: **close, shut**

open adjective

If something is **open** it is not closed or locked.
*"The circus is **open**!" cried the clowns.*

> 1) **ajar** 2) **unlocked** 3) **gaping**

1) *My bedroom door was **ajar**.*
2) *The toy cupboard was **unlocked**.*
3) *The dentist looked into my
   gaping mouth.*

OPEN

Oo order

order verb

To **order** means to command.
*Sergeant Brown **ordered** his soldiers to salute.*

> 1) **command** 2) **direct** 3) **charge** 4) **instruct**

1) *The queen **commanded** everyone to kneel.*
2) *The captain **directed** his crew to abandon ship.*
3) *"I **charge** you to tell the truth!" yelled the judge.*
4) *Mom **instructed** the delivery men to put the bed upstairs.*

ordinary adjective

If something is **ordinary** it is normal or not unexpected.
*Mary wore an **ordinary** coat.*

> 1) **everyday** 2) **normal** 3) **regular** 4) **standard**

1) *A cold is an **everyday** illness.*
2) *The patient's temperature was **normal**.*
3) *I finished school at the **regular** time today.*
4) *A **standard** cup holds eight ounces.*

Opposites: **extraordinary, unusual**

organize verb

To **organize** means to plan something
and work out the details.
*I **organized** the school disco.*

> 1) **arrange** 2) **coordinate** 3) **run**

1) *Uncle Bruno **arranged** a surprise party.*
2) *The police **coordinated** a search of a wide area.*
3) *Miss Block **runs** the town carnival every year.*

out adjective

If you are **out**, you are not at home.
I went to see my best friend but she was ***out***.

> 1) **absent** 2) **away** 3) **elsewhere**

1) *Natalie was* ***absent*** *from school on Monday.*
2) *The gardener went* ***away*** *for two weeks.*
3) *Jake's mom said he was* ***elsewhere*** *with his brother.*

Opposites: **here, in, present**

outside adjective

If something is **outside**, it is away from the inside.
Dad turned on the ***outside*** *faucet.*

> 1) **exterior** 2) **outdoor** 3) **external**

1) *The* ***exterior*** *wall was painted white.*
2) *Mom said football was an* ***outdoor*** *game.*
3) *The* ***external*** *side of the door is scratched.*

Opposite: **inside**

over adjective

If something is **over**, it is in the past.
We got up when the movie was ***over***.

> 1) **finished** 2) **completed** 3) **ended**

1) *We will celebrate when our final exam is* ***finished***.
2) *"Is the test* ***completed***?" asked the scientist.*
3) *When the teacher came in our fun was* ***ended***.

painful adjective

If something is **painful**, it hurts.
*Jason had a really **painful** knee.*

> 1) **aching** 2) **sore** 3) **stinging** 4) **throbbing**

1) *The young athlete's legs were **aching**.*
2) *The skier's bruises were very **sore**.*
3) *The child rubbed her **stinging** eyes.*
4) *"I've got a **throbbing** headache," Bella complained.*

Opposite: **painless**

pale adjective

If something is **pale**, it has little or no color.
*The patient had a **pale** face because she was so ill.*

> 1) **ashen** 2) **colorless** 3) **white**

1) *Her face went **ashen** when she heard the bad news.*
2) *The dying plant's leaves were **colorless**.*
3) *The summer sky was **white** with clouds.*

Opposite: **ruddy**

part noun

A **part** is a section of a whole thing.
*I could only see a **part** of the stage.*

> 1) **piece** 2) **portion** 3) **segment** 4) **fragment**

1) *"Have another **piece** of pizza," said Uncle Roy.*
2) *Marcus saved a **portion** of pie for his brother.*
3) *We shared the **segments** of the orange.*
4) *Only a **fragment** of the original letter from Captain Cook was left.*

pass verb

To **pass** means to move by something.
*I always **pass** the church on my way to school.*

> 1) **go by** 2) **outdo** 3) **outstrip**

1) *I was scared to **go by** the old haunted house.*
2) *I'd like to **outdo** my best score at basketball.*
3) *Zoe **outstripped** all her friends in the hurdles race.*

pass verb

To **pass** means to transfer or exchange an item.
*Jack **passed** the book to his teacher.*

> 1) **give** 2) **hand** 3) **transfer**

1) *"**Give** me that pencil," said Jennifer rudely.*
2) *We **handed** the fossil around the class.*
3) *I **transferred** the problem to my parents.*

patient adjective

If you are **patient**, you do not mind having to wait.
*Miss Brown was **patient** with me when I couldn't do the math problem.*

> 1) **calm** 2) **long-suffering** 3) **untiring** 4) **uncomplaining**

1) *The builder was **calm** when the big beam fell on his foot.*
2) *My **long-suffering** friend always forgives me for being late.*
3) *Marie's work on the difficult problem is **untiring**.*
4) *"You are an **uncomplaining** girl," smiled the doctor.*

Opposite: **impatient**

peaceful adjective

Peaceful means quiet and calm.
*Grandma's garden is a **peaceful** place.*

> 1) **quiet** 2) **restful** 3) **serene**

1) *Libraries are **quiet** places.*
2) *Mom felt better after a **restful** sleep.*
3) *The old woman had a **serene** face.*

Opposites: **disturbed, noisy**

perfect adjective

If something is **perfect**, it has no faults.
*Beth did a **perfect** dive.*

> 1) **faultless** 2) **exact** 3) **flawless** 4) **excellent**

1) *The pianist gave a **faultless** performance at the concert.*
2) *Jill drew an **exact** copy of the picture.*
3) *The **flawless** diamond was worth a fortune.*
4) *My new watch keeps **excellent** time.*

Opposites: **imperfect, wrong**

permission noun

If someone gives you **permission**, that person allows you to do something.
*We had **permission** to visit the Forbidden City in Beijing.*

> 1) **consent** 2) **approval** 3) **agreement**

1) *Dad gave his **consent** for us to stay out late.*
2) *We got **approval** of our plans for building a new house.*
3) *"With your **agreement**, I will make a speech," said Mrs. Carter.*

Opposite: **refusal**

pet noun

A **pet** is a tame animal you keep in your home.
I love taking care of my **pets***.*

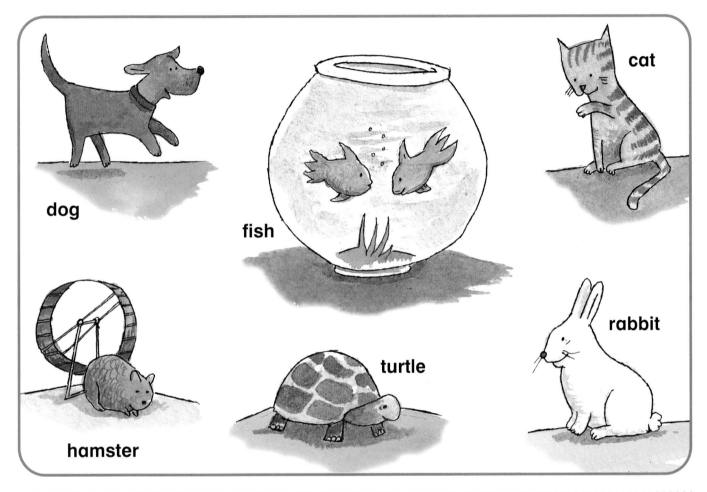

dog

fish

cat

hamster

turtle

rabbit

pick verb

To **pick** means to choose or select.
Ellie was asked to **pick** *players for her team.*

1) **choose** 2) **decide on** 3) **select** 4) **opt for**

1) *Dad always lets Mom* **choose** *the restaurant.*
2) *Daryl* **decided on** *the white sneakers.*
3) *I want to* **select** *a new carpet for my bedroom.*
4) *Greg always* **opts for** *chocolate ice cream.*

Opposite: **reject**

piece noun

A **piece** is a part or a bit of something.
*The waitress gave me a **piece** of apple pie.*

> 1) **bit** 2) **chunk** 3) **scrap** 4) **segment**

1) *The mouse took a **bit** of cheese.*
2) *Daniel handed me a **chunk** of chocolate.*
3) *She picked up a **scrap** of paper from the floor.*
4) *I ate several **segments** of apple during recess.*

pile noun

A **pile** is a heap of something.
*There's a **pile** of dirty clothes in the laundry room.*

> 1) **mound** 2) **mountain** 3) **stack**

1) *There is a **mound** of soil in the garden.*
2) *"I have a **mountain** of homework to do," groaned Violet.*
3) *The doctor had a **stack** of mail in the post each morning.*

place noun

A **place** is a particular area.
*My hometown is an interesting **place**.*

> 1) **spot** 2) **location** 3) **position**

1) *We found a good **spot** to set up our tent.*
2) *Tony's office moved to a new **location** in the city.*
3) *The hiker marked his exact **position** on the map.*

place verb

To **place** means to put.
I placed my books on the shelf.

1) **put** 2) **rest** 3) **lay**

1) *"Please put your litter in the basket,"*
   said the caretaker.
2) *I rested my hands on Clare's shoulders.*
3) *We lay fresh flowers on the grave each week.*

planet noun

We live on a **planet** called Earth.
These are the nine planets in the solar system.

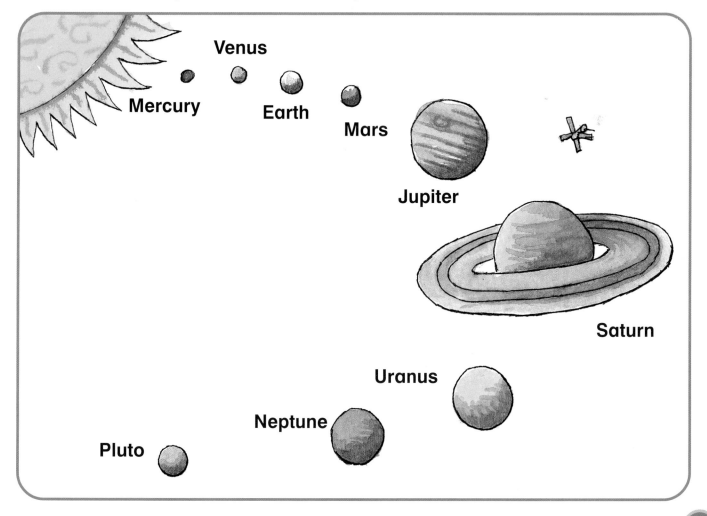

Venus

Mercury   Earth

Mars

Jupiter

Saturn

Uranus

Neptune

Pluto

plant noun

A **plant** is a living thing that puts down roots in the soil and grows.
*I bought a flowering **plant** from the nursery.*

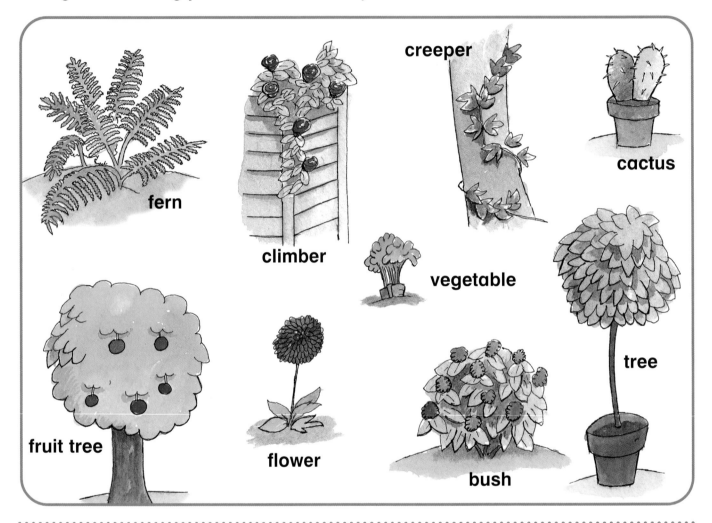

play verb

To **play** means to amuse yourself or to join in a game.
*Peter liked to **play** on his computer.*

> 1) **have fun** 2) **frolic** 3) **romp**

1) *The twins love **having fun** with their friends.*
2) *Lambs **frolic** in the fields in spring.*
3) *The boys like to **romp** in the yard.*

Opposite: **work**

please verb

To **please** someone means to make them happy.
*Philip's kindness **pleased** his mother.*

> 1) **satisfy** 2) **gladden** 3) **thrill**

1) *Eve can never **satisfy** her teacher.*
2) *It **gladdens** me to hear birds singing.*
3) *The ballet dancer **thrilled** the audience
   with her performance.*

Opposite: **displease**

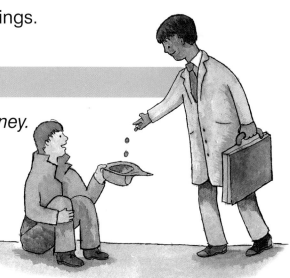

poor adjective

To be **poor** means to have little or no money or things.
*The young beggar was very **poor**.*

> 1) **penniless** 2) **destitute** 3) **needy**

1) *She was **penniless** after giving away all her money.*
2) *The **destitute** family had nowhere to live.*
3) *It is kind to give money to **needy** people.*

Opposites: **rich, wealthy**

pretty adjective

To be **pretty** is to be pleasant to look at.
*Jessica wore a **pretty** dress for the dance.*

> 1) **beautiful** 2) **lovely** 3) **gorgeous** 4) **attractive**

1) *Jill had **beautiful** dark-brown hair.*
2) *Grandma bought some **lovely** silk curtains.*
3) *Mr. and Mrs. Blake lived in a **gorgeous** cottage.*
4) *Jack was an **attractive** boy.*

Opposite: **ugly**

problem noun

A **problem** is a difficulty or question.
*We solved the **problem** of where to hide the treasure.*

> 1) **trouble** 2) **complication** 3) **worry**

1) *"What's the **trouble**?" asked Mom.*
2) *"I'm afraid we have a **complication**," said the engineer.*
3) *Ben's main **worry** was his damaged bike.*

proper adjective

Proper means right for the purpose.
*The **proper** place for an oven is in a kitchen.*

> 1) **correct** 2) **suitable** 3) **fitting**

1) *I put the letters in the **correct** order.*
2) *The library is a **suitable** place to study.*
3) *A shed is not a **fitting** home for a queen.*

Opposites: **improper, wrong**

protect verb

To **protect** means to keep something safe from harm.
*Dad locks his car in the garage to **protect** it from burglars.*

> 1) **defend** 2) **guard** 3) **shelter** 4) **shield**

1) *The soldiers fired arrows to **defend** the castle.*
2) *Special officers **guard** the king and queen.*
3) *The cat **sheltered** her kittens from the rain.*
4) *I **shielded** my friend from the bullies.*

Opposites: **attack, threaten**

proud adjective

To be **proud** means to be pleased with yourself or someone else for doing well.
*Jim was **proud** of himself for earning a swimming award.*

> 1) **boastful** 2) **pleased** 3) **satisfied**

1) *Mr. Green was **boastful** about his smart daughter.*
2) *The students were **pleased** with their test results.*
3) *The pretty girl was **satisifed** with her appearance.*

Opposite: **humble**

pull verb

To **pull** means to drag something or someone toward you.
*The door was stuck, and I had to **pull** hard to open it.*

> 1) **drag** 2) **tow** 3) **haul** 4) **tug**

1) *Beth had to **drag** her heavy bag upstairs.*
2) *Our car **tows** the trailer along the road.*
3) *The teacher **hauled** me out of the pool.*
4) *I had to **tug** at the leash to get my dog to move.*

Opposite: **push**

push verb

To **push** means to force someone or something away from you.
*The fishermen **push** their rowboat into the water.*

> 1) **thrust** 2) **press** 3) **shove**

1) *I **thrust** a dollar into my brother's hand.*
2) *The man had to **press** on the doorbell.*
3) *Mom **shoved** her way to the front of the line.*

Opposite: **pull**

quarrel verb

To **quarrel** means to argue or disagree angrily.
*Sisters often **quarrel** about borrowing each other's clothes.*

> 1) **argue** 2) **disagree** 3) **fight** 4) **squabble**

1) *Tom and Jack **argue** about whose team is best.*
2) *Mom and Dad **disagree** about what color to paint the house.*
3) *I don't like **fighting** with my best friend.*
4) *The children **squabble** over their toys.*

Opposite: **agree**

quest noun

A **quest** is an adventure that involves a search.
*The knight's **quest** was to find the dragon.*

> 1) **hunt** 2) **expedition** 3) **mission**

1) *The prince went on a **hunt** for the princess.*
2) *The aim of their **expedition** was to reach the South Pole.*
3) *Billy's **mission** was to find the lost treasure.*

question verb

To **question** means to ask or inquire.
*The teacher **questioned** us about our vacations.*

> 1) **ask** 2) **interrogate** 3) **quiz**

1) *"I want to **ask** you about this broken window," said our neighbor.*
2) *The police officer **interrogated** his suspect.*
3) *We were **quizzed** about the missing bags.*

quick adjective

If you are **quick**, you are speedy.
*Leroy finished first in the race because he was so **quick**.*

> 1) **swift** 2) **fast** 3) **brisk** 4) **rapid**

1) *Cheetahs are **swift** runners.*
2) *I made a **fast** call before I left the office.*
3) *Dad goes for a **brisk** walk every morning.*
4) *"I am a **rapid** reader," boasted Michelle.*

Opposite: **slow**

quiet adjective

To be **quiet** means to make little or no sound.
*A mouse is a **quiet** animal.*

> 1) **hushed** 2) **noiseless** 3) **silent** 4) **soundless**

1) *People speak in **hushed** voices in church.*
2) *Charlotte tiptoed on **noiseless** feet.*
3) *"Keep **silent**!" ordered Mr. Williams.*
4) *The deer was **soundless** as it ran across the field.*

Opposites: **loud, noisy**

quite adjective

Quite means completely and utterly.
*The magician was **quite** amazing.*

> 1) **absolutely** 2) **completely** 3) **totally** 4) **fully**

1) *I was **absolutely** sure I had the correct answer.*
2) *"I **completely** agree," said the store manager.*
3) *Our crossword answers were **totally** wrong.*
4) *The firefighters were **fully** aware of the risks.*

Rr rain

rain noun

Rain is water that falls from the clouds.
*We went out and danced in the **rain**!*

> 1) **shower** 2) **downpour** 3) **drizzle**

1) *The **shower** did not last long.*
2) *"You're not going out in this **downpour**," said Mom.*
3) *I was on my way home when the **drizzle** began.*

raise verb

To **raise** means to lift upward.
*The nurse had to **raise** Simon's broken leg.*

> 1) **elevate** 2) **escalate** 3) **lift**

1) *If you **elevate** your sprained ankle it will feel better.*
2) *Our local supermarket has **escalated** its prices.*
3) *Beth asked her dad to **lift** her onto his shoulders.*

Opposite: **lower**

ready adjective

If something is **ready**, it is prepared to do something or to be used.
*"Dinner is **ready**!" called Mom.*

> 1) **all set** 2) **primed** 3) **prepared**

1) *We were **all set** to leave until Dad lost the map.*
2) *The class was **primed** for action.*
3) *"Are you **prepared** to face the enemy?" asked the captain.*

Opposites: **unprepared, unready**

real adjective

If something is **real**, it is genuine and not made up.
*Paula's wedding ring had a **real** diamond in it.*

1) **genuine** 2) **true** 3) **honest** 4) **sincere**

1) *The **genuine** princess felt a pea through 100 mattresses.*
2) *My dad is a firefighter and a **true** hero.*
3) *"It was an **honest** mistake!" cried Elaine.*
4) *Michael gave his friends a **sincere** apology.*

Opposite: **fake**

refuse verb

To **refuse** means to say "no."
*The boys **refuse** to eat their dinner.*

1) **decline** 2) **deny** 3) **spurn**

1) *Mary **declined** another cup of tea.*
2) *A guard **denied** us entry to the palace.*
3) *The proud girl **spurned** my help.*

Opposite: **accept**

relax verb

To **relax** means to play or take a rest from work.
*I love to **relax** with a good adventure story.*

1) **unwind** 2) **laze** 3) **rest** 4) **calm down**

1) *I **unwind** by playing chess.*
2) *The dog likes to **laze** on my bed.*
3) *Sean tried to **rest** after working in
   the backyard.*
4) *"I wish you would all **calm down!**"
   said the coach.*

remember verb

If you **remember** something, you keep it in your memory.
*George could not **remember** the way to the bookstore.*

> 1) **recall** 2) **recollect** 3) **call to mind**

1) *Grandpa can **recall** the names of his teachers.*
2) *"I don't **recollect** inviting you," said Peter rudely.*
3) *I can't **call to mind** my friend's address.*

Opposite: **forget**

reptile noun

A **reptile** is a cold-blooded animal with a scaly skin.
*All these are different kinds of **reptile**.*

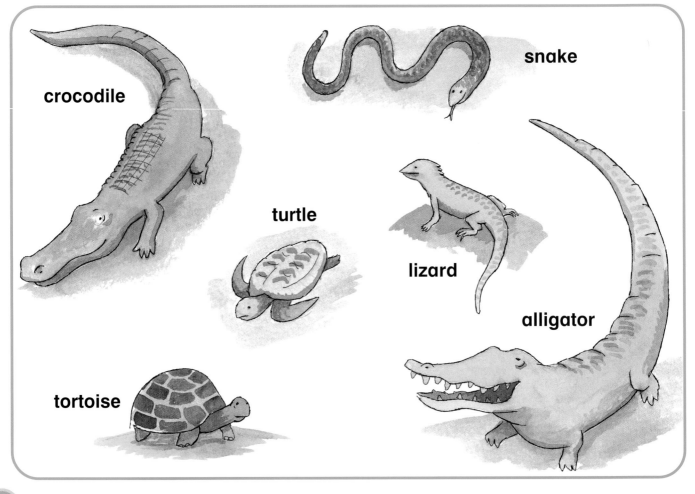

crocodile

snake

turtle

lizard

tortoise

alligator

rescue verb

To **rescue** means to save a person, animal, or thing from danger or harm.
*Jim managed to **rescue** the dog from the lake.*

> 1) **free** 2) **salvage** 3) **save**

1) *The man tried to **free** his friend from the trap.*
2) *We could not **salvage** our furniture from the flood.*
3) *The Coast Guard **saves** the lives of many people every year.*

respect verb

To **respect** someone means to look up to them.
*"You should **respect** your elders," said the old man.*

> 1) **admire** 2) **value** 3) **revere**

1) *Lloyd **admires** his father's courage.*
2) *I **value** my friends' opinions.*
3) *The young sailors **revered** their captain.*

Opposite: **disrespect**

rest noun

A **rest** is a period of relaxing or sleeping.
*Kathleen took a **rest** on the bench.*

> 1) **nap** 2) **sleep** 3) **break**

1) *Grandma takes a **nap** every afternoon.*
2) *The short **sleep** did the toddler good.*
3) *"Take a **break**," said the dancing teacher.*

rest noun

The **rest** is what is left over.
*The bellboy carried three bags and I took the **rest**.*

> 1) **remainder** 2) **surplus** 3) **balance**

1) *I ate the **remainder** of the chocolate cake.*
2) *The **surplus** had to be thrown away after the party.*
3) *The last ship carried the **balance** of the cargo.*

rich adjective

If you are **rich**, you have lots of money
or possessions.
*The **rich** man owned a huge Rolls-Royce car.*

> 1) **wealthy** 2) **affluent** 3) **well-to-do**

1) *A **wealthy** family lives in the huge mansion.*
2) *My aunt is an **affluent** woman.*
3) *The **well-to-do** girls wear expensive clothes.*

Opposite: **poor**

right adjective

If something is **right**, it is correct.
*I hoped I had the **right** answer.*

> 1) **accurate** 2) **correct** 3) **exact** 3) **precise**

1) *The fortune-teller was **accurate**.*
2) *Jane gave the **correct** answer to the question.*
3) *I gave the customer the **exact** change.*
4) *"What is the **precise** time?" asked Ellie.*

Opposite: **wrong**

risk noun

A **risk** is a chance of loss or danger.
*Jacob took a **risk** when he climbed the high wall.*

> 1) **gamble** 2) **chance** 3) **danger** 4) **hazard**

1) *I took a **gamble** and trusted the burglar.*
2) *There was a **chance** that the tires might slip on the ice.*
3) *The factory fire was a **danger** to the houses nearby.*
4) *The flood was a **hazard** to people's safety.*

Opposite: **certainty**

rough adjective

If something is **rough**, it is uneven or harsh to the touch.
*A barnacle has a **rough** surface.*

> 1) **bumpy** 2) **craggy** 3) **stony**

1) *He drove the tractor across the **bumpy** field.*
2) *A puffin perched on the **craggy** cliff.*
3) *The plants could not grow in the **stony** ground.*

Opposite: **smooth**

round adjective

Something that is **round** is shaped like a circle.
*We have a **round** mirror over our fireplace.*

> 1) **circular** 2) **curved** 3) **spiral**

1) *The play was performed on a **circular** stage.*
2) *Natalie has graceful, **curved** handwriting.*
3) *There was a beautiful **spiral** staircase
   in the old mansion.*

row noun

A **row** is a line of people or objects.
There was a row of sunflowers in the garden.

> 1) **chain** 2) **line** 3) **column**

1) *I passed the bucket along the chain of people.*
2) *Margaret has a line of seashells on her windowsill.*
3) *A column of soldiers stood in front of the palace.*

rubbish noun

Rubbish is something you don't need and throw away.
We put our rubbish in the garbage can.

> 1) **litter** 2) **garbage** 3) **trash** 4) **waste**

1) *You should never drop litter on the sidewalk.*
2) *Our garbage is collected by a truck.*
3) *We try to recycle our trash.*
4) *The waste was put in garbage bags.*

rude adjective

If you are **rude**, you are impolite.
The rude girl stuck out her tongue at her friend.

> 1) **bad-mannered** 2) **curt** 3) **surly** 4) **insulting**

1) *The bad-mannered boy shouted at his mom.*
2) *"Shut up!" said Robin in a curt voice.*
3) *I did not like the reporter's surly tone.*
4) *The sergeant spoke in an insulting way.*

Opposite: **polite**

ruin verb

To **ruin** something means to damage it so it can't be fixed.
*The mud on Mickey's boots **ruined** the new carpet.*

> 1) **wreck** 2) **demolish** 3) **destroy** 4) **spoil**

1) *Cindy wanted to **wreck** my stamp collection.*
2) *The waves **demolished** our sand castle.*
3) *The ugly building **destroyed** the beautiful view.*
4) *Sebastian **spoiled** his painting by spilling water on it.*

rule noun

A **rule** is an instruction that tells you what you may or may not do.
*We learned the **rules** before we played the game.*

> 1) **law** 2) **regulation** 3) **decree**

1) *The police make sure that people obey the **law**.*
2) *There are strict **regulations** against cruelty to animals.*
3) *In "Sleeping Beauty" the king makes a **decree** that there are to be no spinning wheels in his kingdom.*

rule verb

To **rule** something means to be in charge of it.
*"I **rule** this kingdom," shouted the bad-tempered king.*

> 1) **control** 2) **govern** 3) **lead** 4) **run**

1) *The pilot **controls** the airplane.*
2) *The new chief **governs** the children's hospital.*
3) *A young woman **leads** the reading group.*
4) *The brothers **run** a little coffee shop.*

rumor noun

A **rumor** is a story passed from one person to another, which may not be true.
*We heard a **rumor** that our history teacher is leaving.*

> 1) **gossip** 2) **talk** 3) **hearsay**

1) *There is a lot of **gossip** about our next-door neighbors.*
2) *"Have you heard all the **talk** about the mayor going to jail?" asked Dad.*
3) *"That story is only **hearsay**," said the TV announcer.*

run verb

To **run** means to move quickly.
*Dad had to **run** to catch the bus.*

> 1) **sprint** 2) **dart** 3) **dash** 4) **scamper**

1) *I can **sprint** faster than all my friends.*
2) *Ben had to **dart** undercover when it started to rain.*
3) *He **dashed** to the store before it closed.*
4) *The kittens **scampered** around the room.*

rush verb

To **rush** means to hurry.
*We had to **rush** to get there on time.*

> 1) **hurry** 2) **fly** 3) **scramble**

1) *Everyone **hurried** home after school.*
2) *"I must **fly**!" panted Mrs. Harris when it started to rain.*
3) *We **scrambled** to be first in line for tickets.*

Opposite: **dawdle**

sad adjective

To be **sad** means to be unhappy.
*Jill was **sad** that she had broken her favorite soft toy.*

1) **unhappy** 2) **miserable** 3) **blue**

1) *Dad was **unhappy** because his car had broken down.*
2) *The girl was **miserable** because her vacation was over.*
3) *Conrad felt **blue** when his dog went missing.*

Opposites: **cheerful, glad, happy**

safe adjective

If something is **safe**, it is free from danger or harm.
*It is **safe** to skate on the ice.*

1) **secure** 2) **protected** 3) **unharmed**

1) *I felt **secure** when all the doors were locked.*
2) *The princess was always **protected** from danger.*
3) *"Make sure the animals are **unharmed**," said the zookeeper.*

Opposites: **dangerous, unsafe**

same adjective

Things that are the **same** are exactly like each other.
*Mary and Jenny wore the **same** dresses.*

1) **alike** 2) **identical** 3) **matching**

1) *My mom and her older sister look **alike**.*
2) *My brother and I are **identical** twins.*
3) *The ski team wore **matching** sweaters.*

Opposite: **different**

Ss save

save verb

To **save** means to store something for use in the future.
*Megan wanted to **save** her money.*

> 1) **keep** 2) **hoard** 3) **hold on to**

1) *I **keep** all my old ticket stubs.*
2) *Misers like to **hoard** their money.*
3) *Tom **held on to** his allowance so he could buy his mom a present.*

Opposites: **spend, waste**

say verb

To **say** means to speak words.
*Jean would not **say** where she had been.*

> 1) **utter** 2) **state** 3) **remark** 4) **exclaim**

1) *The stranger did not **utter** a word.*
2) *"Please **state** your name," said the judge.*
3) *The babysitter **remarked** that it was bedtime.*
4) *"Leave me alone!" I **exclaimed**.*

scare verb

To **scare** means to frighten.
*Billy put on a vampire mask to **scare** me.*

> 1) **alarm** 2) **terrify** 3) **startle**

1) *"Don't **alarm** Grandma by shouting," warned Dad.*
2) *Fireworks **terrify** my pet cat.*
3) *I was **startled** by the loud bang.*

scream verb

To **scream** means to yell loudly.
*Annette **screamed** when she saw the ghost.*

> 1) **yell** 2) **screech** 3) **shriek**

1) *I **yelled** as the car rolled backwards.*
2) *"Don't **screech** in my ear!" complained Mom.*
3) *The sick baby **shrieked** for hours.*

seat noun

A **seat** is something made to sit on.
*My favorite **seat** is soft and cozy.*

easy chair

sofa

dining chair

stool

throne

beach chair

bench

secret adjective

If something is **secret**, it is not to be told or shown to others.
*We have a **secret** club.*

> 1) **private** 2) **concealed** 3) **hidden** 4) **unknown**

1) *I write my **private** thoughts in my diary.*
2) *"I'll put your jewels in the **concealed** safe," said the manager.*
3) *The desk has a **hidden** compartment.*
4) *Collette's **unknown** admirer sent her red roses.*

see verb

To **see** means to observe with your eyes.
*I can **see** the mountains from my bedroom window.*

> 1) **glimpse** 2) **spot** 3) **witness**

1) *Rosina did not **glimpse** any fairies.*
2) *"Did you **spot** the butterfly?" asked Mom eagerly.*
3) *I **witnessed** the rail accident.*

selfish ajective

To be **selfish** means to think only about your own needs and wishes.
*It was **selfish** of Owen to drink all the water.*

> 1) **greedy** 2) **self-centered** 3) **ungenerous**

1) *The **greedy** woman left no food for the children.*
2) *We taught our **self-centered** friend a lesson.*
3) *An **ungenerous** person had taken the last blanket.*

Opposite: **generous**

send verb

To **send** something means to direct it to another place.
*Daisy had to **send** a letter to her friend Sarah.*

> 1) **mail** 2) **dispatch** 3) **forward** 4) **transmit**

1) *I **mail** a letter to my aunt once a week.*
2) *People **dispatch** thousands of packages every day.*
3) *My boss asked me to **forward** his mail to him.*
4) *Diana **transmits** emails to all her friends.*

Opposite: **receive**

sensible adjective

If something is **sensible**, it is wise.
*It is **sensible** to wear warm clothes in the winter.*

> 1) **wise** 2) **practical** 3) **reasonable**

1) *The professor always gives **wise** advice.*
2) *The builder had some **practical** ideas.*
3) *It was **reasonable** to ask for a lunch break.*

Opposites: **silly, unwise**

serious adjective

If something is **serious**, it is important or worrying.
*Everyone looks very **serious** in the old photo.*

> 1) **grave** 2) **solemn** 3) **long-faced**

1) *Dad looked **grave** when he told us the bad news.*
2) *We were very **solemn** when we met the judge.*
3) *The **long-faced** man did not laugh at the joke.*

Opposite: **lighthearted**

shake verb

To **shake** means to move quickly up and down or back and forth.
The heavy dinosaur made the earth **shake** *when it moved.*

> 1) **quiver** 2) **shiver** 3) **shudder** 4) **tremble**

1) *I saw the leaves* **quiver** *in the breeze.*
2) *Most people* **shiver** *if they are cold.*
3) *Scary stories can make you* **shudder**.
4) *The little dog* **trembled** *with fear.*

shape noun

The **shape** of something is the form you make if you draw a line around its outside edges.
An orange has a round **shape**.

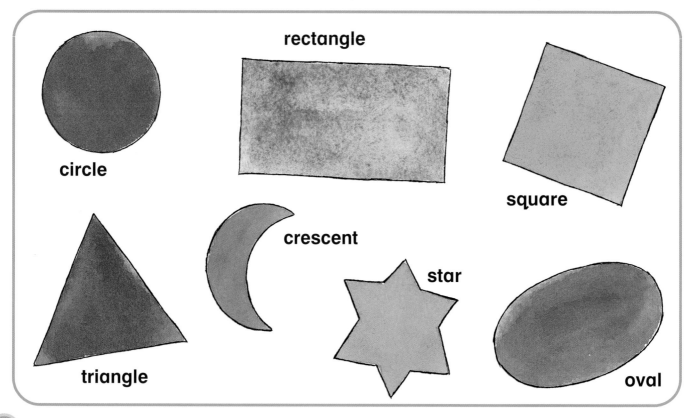

circle

rectangle

square

crescent

star

triangle

oval

share verb

To **share** means to divide something between a number of people.
*We **shared** our food on the camping trip.*

> 1) **divide** 2) **split** 3) **distribute**

1) *Dad **divided** the prize money between us.*
2) *I **split** the cake into four equal pieces.*
3) *The jobs were **distributed** among the three men.*

sharp adjective

If something is **sharp**, it is pointed and could cut you.
*The **sharp** scissors cut through the paper.*

> 1) **pointy** 2) **keen** 3) **cutting**

1) *The seamstress pricked her finger on the **pointy** needle.*
2) *The pirate captain's sword had a **keen** blade.*
3) *"The **cutting** edge of a knife is dangerous,"
said the cook.*

Opposite: **blunt**

shine verb

If something **shines**, it glows brightly.
*My silver ring **shines** in the sun.*

> 1) **beam** 2) **gleam** 3) **glitter** 4) **sparkle**

1) *The moonlight **beams** through my curtains.*
2) *A light was **gleaming** in the library window.*
3) *The little girl's eyes **glittered** with excitement.*
4) *The sunlight **sparkled** on the water.*

shoe noun

A **shoe** is a covering you wear on your foot.
*"Put your **shoes** on before you go out," said Dad.*

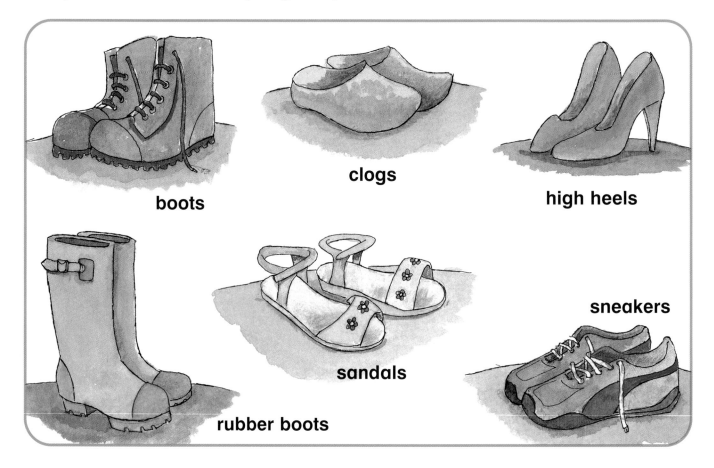

boots

clogs

high heels

rubber boots

sandals

sneakers

short adjective

Something **short** is less than usual height or length.
*The carpenter picked up a **short** plank of wood.*

1) **little** 2) **small** 3) **squat**

1) *I bought a **little** tree to plant in my garden.*
2) *"You are too **small** to go on that ride,"
the man told Jamie.*
3) *Our neighbor is a **squat** woman.*

Opposites: **long, tall**

shout verb

To **shout** means to call out loudly.
*Ben had to **shout** to make his friend hear.*

> 1) **bellow** 2) **yell** 3) **bawl** 4) **roar**

1) *The coach had to **bellow** at the players.*
2) *Dad began to **yell** when his team scored.*
3) *I **bawled** at my friend across the playground.*
4) *"Don't do that!" **roared** the teacher.*

Opposite: **whisper**

show verb

To **show** means to allow something to be seen.
*The soldiers were proud to **show** their medals to us.*

> 1) **reveal** 2) **display** 3) **present**

1) *I pulled off my mask to **reveal** my face.*
2) *Maggie **displays** her sculptures in the art gallery.*
3) *The lawyer **presents** her evidence to the jury.*

Opposite: **hide**

shy adjective

A **shy** person is nervous with strangers.
*My **shy** cousin blushed when I spoke to her.*

> 1) **timid** 2) **bashful** 3) **meek**

1) *The **timid** dog put his tail between his legs.*
2) *Lewis was **bashful** around girls.*
3) *The new recruit spoke in a **meek** voice.*

Opposite: **outgoing**

silent adjective

To be **silent** means to make no noise.
*The manager was **silent** while she listened
to our complaint.*

> 1) **quiet** 2) **noiseless** 3) **soundless**

1) *"Be **quiet**!" snapped the marshal.*
2) *The burglars were **noiseless** when they
   broke into the house.*
3) *Roland danced on **soundless** feet.*

Opposite: **noisy**

silly adjective

If something is **silly**, it is not sensible.
*Dad told us to stop being **silly**.*

> 1) **absurd** 2) **foolish** 3) **idiotic** 4) **unwise**

1) *"That's an **absurd** idea!" laughed Sonia.*
2) *The clowns played **foolish** games.*
3) *Our **idiotic** dog loves chasing his own tail.*
4) *It is **unwise** to trust a liar.*

Opposites: **sensible, wise**

simple adjective

If something is **simple**, it is easy to do or understand.
*Beth liked doing **simple** math problems.*

> 1) **easy** 2) **clear** 3) **plain**

1) *Our chemistry teacher showed us an **easy** way to do the experiment.*
2) *"The answer is **clear**," said the senator.*
3) *It was **plain** to see who was in charge.*

Opposites: **complicated, difficult**

sleep verb

When you **sleep**, you close your eyes and rest.
*I can't **sleep** with the light on.*

> 1) **nap** 2) **snooze** 3) **doze** 4) **slumber**

1) *Grandpa likes to **nap** in the sun.*
2) *Cats **snooze** whenever they can.*
3) *The baby **dozed** in his crib.*
4) *Dad **slumbered** while we watched a film.*

Opposite: **awaken**

slide verb

To **slide** means to move slowly along a surface.
*It is fun to **slide** on the ice.*

> 1) **glide** 2) **skate** 3) **slip** 4) **skid**

1) *The dancers **glide** across the floor.*
2) *I love to **skate** at the ice rink.*
3) *"Dad **slipped** on a banana skin," giggled Suzy.*
4) *We **skid** on the kitchen floor when it has been polished.*

slow adjective

If something is **slow**, it takes a long time.
*Tortoises are **slow** walkers.*

> 1) **lazy** 2) **plodding** 3) **leisurely**

1) *Mrs. Hawkins is a **lazy** worker.*
2) *The man walked with **plodding** steps.*
3) *We took a **leisurely** stroll to the store.*

Opposites: **fast, quick**

small adjective

If something is **small**, it is little or tiny.
*The **small** boy could not reach the book from the shelf.*

> 1) **little** 2) **miniature** 3) **tiny**

1) *The baby wore **little** mittens.*
2) *I bought a **miniature** table for my doll house.*
3) *A bumblebee has **tiny** wings.*

Opposites: **big, huge, large**

smell noun

A **smell** is something that your nose detects.
*I held my nose to keep out the fishy **smell**.*

> 1) **odor** 2) **scent** 3) **fragrance** 4) **aroma**

1) *The sweaty sneakers had a horrible **odor**.*
2) *Dogs can track people by following their **scent**.*
3) *Flowers give off a lovely **fragrance**.*
4) *"What a wonderful **aroma**!" cried the hungry man.*

smooth adjective

If something is **smooth**, it has no bumps or roughness.
*A squash ball has a **smooth** surface.*

> 1) **glossy** 2) **polished** 3) **shiny** 4) **sleek**

1) *I wrote my invitations on **glossy** paper.*
2) *Dad gave the table a **polished** finish.*
3) *My sister has lovely, **shiny** hair.*
4) *I like to stroke my cat's **sleek** coat.*

Opposites: **coarse, rough**

soft adjective

If something is **soft**, it is easy to dent it or change its shape.
*We made cookies with the **soft** dough.*

> 1) **spongy** 2) **cushiony** 3) **flexible**

1) *I bounced on the **spongy** mattress.*
2) *Anthony sank into the **cushiony** easy chair.*
3) *The man heated the glass until it was **flexible**.*

Opposite: **hard**

sorry adjective

If you are **sorry**, you feel bad about something you
have said or done.
*"I'm **sorry** I broke the vase," said Kitty.*

> 1) **apologetic** 2) **ashamed** 3) **regretful** 4) **remorseful**

1) *The waiter was **apologetic** about the horrible food.*
2) *We felt **ashamed** that we had not believed our friend.*
3) *I am **regretful** that I lost my temper.*
4) *The **remorseful** bully asked us to forgive him.*

Opposite: **remorseless**

sort noun

A **sort** is a brand, a group, or a kind.
*"What **sort** of soda should we buy?" I asked.*

> 1) **type** 2) **kind** 3) **brand**

1) *Colin likes all **types** of music.*
2) *We saw many **kinds** of bird on our walk.*
3) *I always use the same **brand** of toothpaste.*

spare adjective

If something is **spare**, it is extra or more than is needed.
*There was a **spare** seat next to me in the theater.*

1) **additional** 2) **extra** 3) **leftover**

1) *We had five **additional** tickets.*
2) *"Who would like the **extra** mushrooms?" asked Dad.*
3) *There were six **leftover** glasses.*

speak verb

To **speak** means to talk.
*Matilda's best friend would not **speak** to her.*

1) **talk** 2) **chat** 3) **converse**

1) *You should not **talk** in assembly.*
2) *I **chat** to my friends on the phone for hours.*
3) *Joseph enjoys **conversing** with his grandpa.*

special adjective

If something is **special**, it is important and unusual.
*Eliza won a very **special** prize in the competition.*

1) **significant** 2) **important** 3) **unique**

1) *Your birthday is a **significant** day.*
2) *"You are very **important** to me," Hugh said.*
3) *The ancient vase was a **unique** design.*

Opposites: **common, ordinary**

speed verb

To **speed** means to move very quickly.
I always speed home from school.

> 1) **race** 2) **hurry** 3) **rush** 4) **zoom**

1) *Polly had to **race** to be on time.*
2) *"**Hurry** up and get changed,"
said the sports teacher.*
3) *The fans **rushed** to see the movie star.*
4) *We **zoomed** down the road on our rollerblades.*

Opposite: **crawl**

spin verb

To **spin** means to turn around very quickly.
When I spin around I get dizzy.

> 1) **twirl** 2) **whirl** 3) **revolve**

1) *Jasmine **twirled** to show off her new dress.*
2) *The fallen leaves **whirled** in the strong wind.*
3) *The hotel doors **revolve** to let people in and out.*

spoil verb

To **spoil** something means to ruin it.
The wind spoiled Jessica's hairdo.

> 1) **ruin** 2) **damage** 3) **wreck** 4) **destroy**

1) *Grass stains **ruined** my new dress.*
2) *Too much water can **damage** plants.*
3) *A terrible storm **wrecked** our garden.*
4) *"I'm going to **destroy** your art work," snarled the protester.*

sport noun

A **sport** is a game you play to win or to have fun.
*My brother plays **sport** at school on Mondays.*

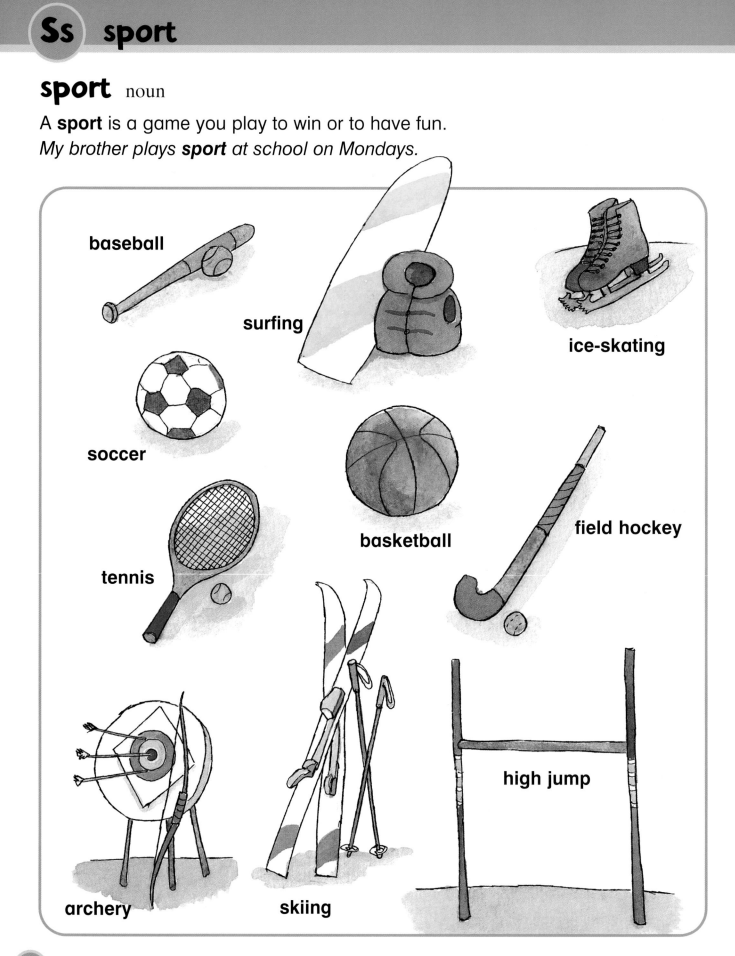

baseball

surfing

ice-skating

soccer

basketball

field hockey

tennis

archery

skiing

high jump

start verb

To **start** something is to begin it or make it begin.
*At the **start** of the race Jack was in the lead.*

> 1) **begin** 2) **open** 3) **set up**

1) *"**Begin** on page five," said the teacher.*
2) *She **opened** the game by throwing out the first ball.*
3) *My cousin **set up** the school drama club.*

Opposites: **end, finish**

stay verb

To **stay** means to remain.
*Fred had to **stay** inside because he had a cold.*

> 1) **remain** 2) **settle** 3) **linger**

1) *It started to rain so we **remained** in the car.*
2) *The family decided to **settle** in Canada.*
3) *My sister wants to **linger** with me.*

Opposites: **go, leave**

stop verb

To **stop** something means to end it.
*Dad could not **stop** us from arguing.*

> 1) **cease** 2) **finish** 3) **halt**

1) *The noise **ceased** at midnight.*
2) *I **finish** work at five every day.*
3) *The police officer tried to **halt** the traffic.*

Opposite: **start**

story noun

A **story** is a description of real or made-up events.
Patrick did not believe his friend's story.

> 1) **tale** 2) **account** 3) **fairy tale** 4) **legend**

1) *The class listened to the exciting **tale**.*
2) *I gave my **account** of what had happened.*
3) *"Read me a **fairy tale**," begged the little girl.*
4) *We like to hear about the **legend** of Robin Hood.*

strange adjective

If something is **strange**, it is odd or unusual.
*There was a **strange** smell coming from the oven.*

> 1) **curious** 2) **weird** 3) **odd** 4) **peculiar**

1) *Grandpa told us a **curious** story.*
2) *"Can you hear that **weird** noise?" asked Harriet.*
3) *The man had an **odd** way of walking.*
4) *John got a **peculiar** letter in the mail.*

Opposites: **common, ordinary, usual**

strict adjective

To be **strict** means to be severe about obeying the rules.
*Our teacher is **strict** but fair.*

> 1) **firm** 2) **severe** 3) **stern** 4) **harsh**

1) *The library has **firm** rules about how many books you can borrow.*
2) *The old lady's **severe** expression scared George.*
3) *The **stern** coach would not let anyone talk during football practice.*
4) *Mandy was upset by her brother's **harsh** words.*

strong adjective

To be **strong** means to have great power or force.
Uncle Ernie is a strong man.

> 1) **tough** 2) **stout** 3) **sturdy**

1) *"I'm as tough as iron!" grinned Dad.*
2) *A swing dangled from the stout tree in our yard.*
3) *The sturdy boy carried his bike across the stream.*

Opposite: **weak**

stupid adjective

To be **stupid** means to be unintelligent.
The stupid boy put his head in a lion's mouth.

> 1) **brainless** 2) **dense** 3) **dim** 4) **foolish**

1) *Our brainless dog thinks he's a pig.*
2) *Dylan is dense when it comes to history.*
3) *The cat is dim but we love him.*
4) *Crossing against the light is a foolish thing to do.*

Opposites: **clever, intelligent, smart**

sudden adjective

If something is **sudden**, it is fast or not expected.
My sudden movement scared the feeding birds.

> 1) **abrupt** 2) **surprising** 3) **quick** 4) **unexpected**

1) *The ballet came to an abrupt end when the stage collapsed.*
2) *The mystery story had a surprising twist at the end.*
3) *The car took a quick right turn.*
4) *An unexpected visitor arrived at the house.*

Opposite: **gradual**

sulk verb

To **sulk** is to be quiet because you are angry or in a bad mood.
*You shouldn't **sulk** just because you didn't win the game.*

> 1) **brood** 2) **mope** 3) **scowl**

1) *Anna couldn't stop **brooding** about her silly mistake.*
2) *My brother just **mopes** around the house all day.*
3) *Sarah **scowled** when Dad didn't give her any candy.*

sure adjective

If something is **sure**, it is not in doubt.
*The racehorse was a **sure** winner.*

> 1) **certain** 2) **positive** 3) **definite**

1) *The farmer was **certain** that his bull had won first prize.*
2) *The old woman was **positive** she had seen the doctor before.*
3) *Fred had a **definite** reason for wanting to go on the school trip.*

surprise noun

A **surprise** is something you did not expect.
*My birthday party was a big **surprise**.*

> 1) **shock** 2) **blow** 3) **bombshell** 4) **jolt**

1) *It was a **shock** to see all the storm damage.*
2) *Failing the French test was a **blow** for Meg.*
3) *Emma's news about her move was a **bombshell**.*
4) *The movie's unexpected ending gave the audience a **jolt**.*

take verb

To **take** means to get hold of something.
*The bullies **take** Bobby's lunch money.*

> 1) **seize** 2) **grasp** 3) **clutch**

1) *I **seized** the oars and rowed away.*
2) *"Try to **grasp** the rope!" shouted the climber.*
3) *The nervous girl **clutched** her father's hand.*

Opposite: **give**

talk verb

To **talk** means to say words.
*We were told not to **talk** in class.*

> 1) **chat** 2) **speak** 3) **tell**

1) *We **chatted** all the way home.*
2) *"Don't **speak** to anyone you don't know," said my dad.*
3) *My best friend came over to **tell** me about the party.*

No talking in class!

tall adjective

To be **tall** means to be above normal height.
*Peter was **tall** for his age.*

> 1) **big** 2) **high** 3) **lanky** 4) **towering**

1) *The **big** boys played on the football team.*
2) *The **high** wall was hard to climb.*
3) *Leo was a **lanky** teenager.*
4) *The **towering** building seemed to touch the clouds.*

Opposites: **low, short, small**

teacher noun

A **teacher** is someone whose job is helping others to learn.
*Miss Brooks is our new **teacher**.*

> 1) **instructor** 2) **tutor** 3) **professor**

1) *I was scared of skiing, but my **instructor** helped me.*
2) *Kara had a private **tutor** to teach her advanced math.*
3) *"Pay attention in class!" shouted the **professor**.*

tear verb

To **tear** means to rip.
*I didn't mean to **tear** my new pants.*

> 1) **rip** 2) **slit** 3) **split**

1) *Nicholas **ripped** his father's travel diary.*
2) *The thorns **slit** holes in my jacket.*
3) *"You've **split** your top," said the dressmaker.*

tell verb

To **tell** means to give information in words.
*Annie and Amy like to **tell** each other secrets.*

> 1) **announce** 2) **confess** 3) **state** 4) **notify**

1) *Matthew and Emma wanted to **announce** their engagement.*
2) *The accused decided to **confess** the truth.*
3) *The witness had to **state** how the accident happened.*
4) *"Please **notify** me when you feel better," said the doctor.*

temper noun

A **temper** is an angry mood.
*Lisa frowns when she is in a **temper**.*

1) **rage** 2) **tantrum** 3) **fury**

1) *Our teacher was in a **rage** because we were late.*
2) *My naughty little brother threw a **tantrum**.*
3) *My mom flew into a **fury** when she saw my bedroom.*

thankful adjective

If you are **thankful**, you are grateful.
*Beth was **thankful** that Aunt Aggie remembered her birthday.*

1) **appreciative** 2) **grateful** 3) **relieved**

1) *Mom was **appreciative** of our help when we went camping.*
2) *Grandma was **grateful** to get the box of plums.*
3) *"We're **relieved** that we've passed our exams," said the students.*

Opposites: **thankless, unappreciative, ungrateful**

thick adjective

To be **thick** means to be large in width or depth.
*The room was covered in a **thick** layer of dust.*

1) **broad** 2) **wide** 3) **deep**

1) *The wrestler puffed out his **broad** chest.*
2) *My sister drew a **wide** line across our bedroom floor.*
3) *We walked through the **deep** blanket of snow.*

Opposite: **thin**

thin adjective

To be **thin** means to be small in width or depth.
*My cousin Alice is tall and very **thin**.*

> 1) **skinny** 2) **slender** 3) **lean** 4) **slim**

1) *"You are too **skinny**," said Dr. Hurst.*
2) *A breeze shook the **slender** tree.*
3) *The stray dog was scruffy and **lean**.*
4) *Brian gave his girlfriend a **slim** book of poetry.*

Opposites: **fat, thick**

thing noun

Thing is a word to describe any object that is not alive.
*"What is that **thing**?" asked Lara.*

> 1) **article** 2) **object** 3) **item**

1) *The fishermen threw some **articles** into the ocean.*
2) *I did not know what the stone **objects** in the museum were.*
3) *The strange **items** glowed in the dark.*

think verb

To **think** means to form ideas in your mind.
*John tried hard to **think** of an answer.*

> 1) **ponder** 2) **consider** 3) **reason** 4) **muse**

1) *The poet sat down to **ponder**.*
2) *I did not **consider** that I was wrong.*
3) *The hikers **reasoned** they should go south.*
4) *"There can only be one answer,"*
   ***mused** the detective.*

throw verb

To **throw** means to send something through the air using your arm and hand.
*The new pitcher can **throw** a ball a long way.*

> 1) **fling** 2) **hurl** 3) **toss** 4) **pitch**

1) *I was told to **fling** the confetti at the bride.*
2) *"Don't **hurl** crayons across the room!" said Miss Frost.*
3) *The baby **tossed** her rattle out of the stroller.*
4) *The captain **pitched** a fly ball.*

Opposite: **catch**

thud noun

A **thud** is the sound of something heavy hitting a surface.
*The rider hit the ground with a **thud**.*

> 1) **bang** 2) **clunk** 3) **thump**

1) *There was a loud **bang** when the worker dropped his hammer.*
2) *A noisy **clunk** made everyone jump.*
3) *Jill fell to the floor with a **thump**.*

tidy adjective

Tidy means neat and in order.
*My brother has a **tidy** bedroom.*

> 1) **neat** 2) **orderly** 3) **well-kept**

1) *Alana's clothes are **neat** and clean.*
2) *Mr. Lee has an **orderly** classroom.*
3) *Lots of visitors came to see the **well-kept** gardens.*

Opposites: **messy, untidy**

tight adjective

If something is **tight**, it fits with no room to spare.
*The young skier wore a **tight** jacket.*

> 1) **close-fitting** 2) **cramped** 3) **snug**

1) *I chose a **close-fitting** sweater.*
2) *Space was **cramped** in the crowded train.*
3) *Gail's shoes were a bit too **snug**.*

Opposite: **loose**

tiny adjective

If something is **tiny**, it is very small.
*I saw a **tiny** mouse on top of the cupboard.*

> 1) **little** 2) **minute** 3) **small**

1) *The children love their **little** rabbit.*
2) *Hazel was scared of the **minute** spider.*
3) *The woodsman had a **small** cut on his hand.*

Opposites: **big, huge, large**

tired adjective

If you are **tired**, you feel that you need
to rest.
*The soldiers were too **tired** to keep marching.*

> 1) **exhausted** 2) **weary** 3) **worn out** 3) **sleepy**

1) *The **exhausted** children went to sleep early.*
2) *"You look **weary**," said Mom.*
3) *I was **worn out** from running the race.*
4) *We were too **sleepy** to watch the late film.*

Opposites: **energetic, fresh**

tool noun

A **tool** is an instrument you use to help you do a job.
*A rake is a gardening **tool**.*

spade

ax

hammer

fork

screwdriver

hoe

wrench

rake

electric drill

saw

top noun

The **top** is the highest part.
*Freddy climbed to the **top** of the mountain.*

1) **tip** 2) **crown** 3) **peak**

1) *The **tip** of the iceberg poked out of the ocean.*
2) *Dad is going bald at the **crown** of his head.*
3) *The climber reached the mountain's **peak**.*

Opposites: **base, bottom**

topic noun

A **topic** is a subject.
*"Today's **topic** is underwater life," said Mr. Wells.*

> 1) **subject** 2) **theme** 3) **issue**

1) *The students had a choice of three **subjects**.*
2) *Magic was the **theme** of Lauren's story.*
3) *Everyone at the meeting wanted to discuss a different **issue**.*

total adjective

If something is **total**, it is complete.
*Our school play was a **total** success.*

> 1) **complete** 2) **absolute** 3) **utter**

1) *"You are a **complete** idiot,"
   said Nicole.*
2) *The game was an **absolute** bore.*
3) *My grandpa is an **utter** genius.*

Opposite: **partial**

total noun

The **total** is the sum of several amounts added together.
*I counted the money and worked out the **total**.*

> 1) **amount** 2) **entirety** 3) **sum**

1) *The **amount** was enough to buy a car.*
2) *We emptied our piggy banks and
   gave the **entirety** to charity.*
3) *I added the numbers and showed
   the **sum** to my teacher.*

touch verb

To **touch** something means to feel it.
*Mark had to **touch** the button to make the lamp work.*

> 1) **handle** 2) **feel** 3) **pat**

1) *When I **handled** the vase I broke it.*
2) *Courtney reached out to **feel** the dress.*
3) *Mom said I could **pat** the dog.*

tough adjective

To be **tough** means to be strong and sturdy.
*Soldiers have to be brave and **tough**.*

> 1) **hardy** 2) **brawny** 3) **sturdy**

1) *The **hardy** tents kept out the rain.*
2) *"I need a **brawny** helper to carry this box," said Miss Robson.*
3) *There is a **sturdy** table in our playroom.*

Opposite: **weak**

trap verb

To **trap** something means to catch or hold it so that it cannot escape.
*The cruel boy **trapped** a wasp under a glass.*

> 1) **capture** 2) **catch** 3) **corner**

1) *The rangers tried to **capture** the lion.*
2) *We tried to **catch** the runaway mouse.*
3) *The officers **cornered** the robbers.*

Opposite: **release**

travel verb

To **travel** means to go from one place to another.
*I have to **travel** for two hours to see my uncle.*

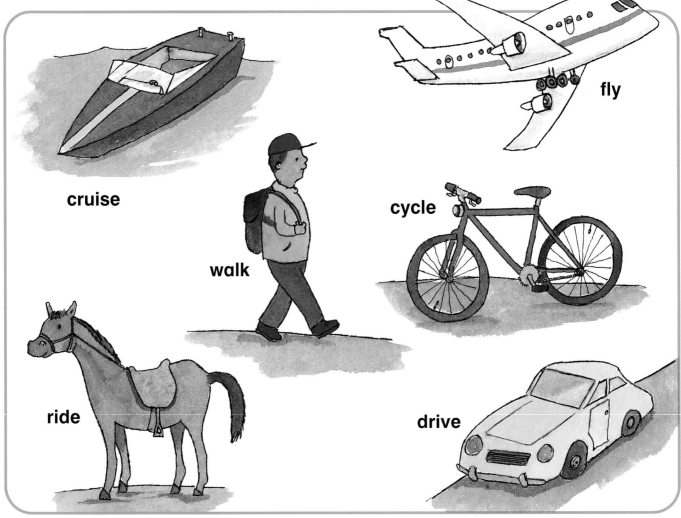

cruise

fly

walk

cycle

ride

drive

treasure noun

Treasure is something of great value or worth.
*The pirates' **treasure** was gold and jewels.*

> 1) **wealth** 2) **fortune** 3) **riches**

1) *"I will give away my **wealth**,"*
   said the generous woman.
2) *The gambler lost his family **fortune**.*
3) *The millionaire hid his **riches** in a safe.*

treat verb

How you **treat** someone is how you behave toward that person.
*Kyle's foster parents **treat** him well.*

> 1) **deal with** 2) **handle** 3) **use**

1) *"I **deal with** every player fairly," said the umpire.*
2) *Dr. Morgan **handles** her patients with kindness.*
3) *"**Use** the lab equipment carefully," said our teacher.*

trick verb

To **trick** someone is to fool them or play a joke on them.
*Rob **tricked** his mom into answering the doorbell.*

> 1) **fool** 2) **deceive** 3) **cheat**

1) *Jennifer **fooled** me into thinking I had won a big prize.*
2) *A dishonest salesclerk **deceived** her by selling a fake diamond ring.*
3) *He won the card game by **cheating** when no one was looking.*

true noun

If something is **true**, it is real or factual.
*Everything the reporter said was **true**.*

> 1) **correct** 2) **genuine** 3) **real**

1) *Only I knew the **correct** answer.*
2) *Wesley has a **genuine** love of snakes.*
3) *The spy told no one his **real** name.*

Opposites: **false, untrue**

trust verb

To **trust** someone means to have confidence in them.
*I **trust** all my friends to tell me the truth.*

> 1) **believe** 2) **count on** 3) **depend on**

1) *The store manager **believed** the customer when no one else did.*
2) *"Can I **count on** you to keep a secret?" asked Chloe.*
3) *You can never **depend on** my sister to be on time.*

Opposite: **mistrust**

try verb

To **try** something means to make an effort to do it.
*Jacob wants to **try** to learn to dive.*

> 1) **aim** 2) **attempt** 3) **strive**

1) *Our team captain always **aims** to win.*
2) *The climbers will **attempt** to climb the highest peak in the mountain range.*
3) *Good competitors always **strive** to do their best.*

turn verb

To **turn** means to move in a circular direction.
*The wheels **turn** to make the car move.*

> 1) **revolve** 2) **rotate** 3) **spin** 4) **pivot**

1) *The model **revolved** to face the artist.*
2) *The planets **rotate** around the sun.*
3) *Some performers can **spin** plates on sticks.*
4) *A basketball player **pivots** on the spot.*

ugly adjective

If something is **ugly**, it is not nice to look at.
*Everyone was scared of the **ugly** witch.*

> 1) **homely** 2) **hideous** 3) **unattractive**

1) *"You are a **homely** girl," said the woman rudely.*
2) *The monster had a **hideous** face.*
3) *Laura wore an **unattractive** coat.*

Opposites: **beautiful, pretty**

uncover verb

To **uncover** something means to take the cover off it or show it to others.
*The chef **uncovered** the pan.*

> 1) **expose** 2) **reveal** 3) **unmask**

1) *I pulled off the cloth to **expose** the table.*
2) *The detective wanted to **reveal** the truth.*
3) *The security guard **unmasked** the real thief.*

Opposites: **conceal, cover, hide**

under preposition

If something is **under**, it is below.
*The farmer put the newborn lamb **under** his coat to keep it warm.*

> 1) **below** 2) **beneath** 3) **underneath**

1) *Alfred put the basket **below** the stairs.*
2) *The old woman hid the dog **beneath** her chair.*
3) *"Put the box **underneath** the table," said Miss Fox.*

understand verb

To **understand** something is to know what it means.
*My cousin Ernest can **understand** French.*

> 1) **grasp** 2) **know** 3) **get**

1) *The pilot tried to **grasp** the meaning of the message from the control tower.*
2) *Tom and Tim **know** how airplanes work.*
3) *The new student did not **get** the joke.*

Opposite: **misunderstand**

Bonjour!

undo verb

To **undo** means to loosen or untie.
*Dad wanted to **undo** the parcel quickly.*

> 1) **untie** 2) **open** 3) **unbutton**

1) *I started to **untie** the knots.*
2) *Someone has already **opened** the box.*
3) *The doctor **unbuttoned** his coat.*

Opposites: **fasten, tie**

unfair adjective

If something is **unfair**, it is not right or equal.
*Todd is an **unfair** player who always cheats.*

> 1) **unjust** 2) **biased** 3) **one-sided** 4) **prejudiced**

1) *The prisoner was given an **unjust** sentence.*
2) *The driver wrote a **biased** report about the accident.*
3) *The general gave a **one-sided** account of the enemy's attack.*
4) *Mr. Jones has a **prejudiced** view of teenagers.*

unfold verb

To **unfold** means to open up or spread out.
*Mom asked Liam to **unfold** the sheets.*

> 1) **unfurl** 2) **open** 3) **spread out**

1) *The explorers **unfurled** their country's flag.*
2) *Ben couldn't wait to **open** his presents.*
3) *The navigator **spread out** the map to check their position.*

Opposite: **fold**

unhappy adjective

If you are **unhappy**, you feel sad.
*Josh was **unhappy** when his model plane broke.*

> 1) **dismal** 2) **downcast** 3) **miserable** 4) **sad**

1) *Faith was **dismal** after her grandparents left.*
2) *He was **downcast** because he did not make the team.*
3) *The **miserable** woman never seemed to smile.*
4) *The girl was **sad** because her best friend had moved away.*

Opposites: **glad, happy**

unkind adjective

If someone is **unkind**, that person causes
pain and sadness to others.
*It is **unkind** to tease shy people.*

> 1) **cruel** 2) **nasty** 3) **mean** 4) **spiteful**

1) *The **cruel** man left his dog out in the rain.*
2) *"Don't be so **nasty**!" sobbed Helena.*
3) *I don't like it when people are **mean** to me.*
4) *Our neighbor was a **spiteful** person.*

Opposite: **kind**

unknown adjective

If something is **unknown**, it is not part
of someone's knowledge.
*An **unknown** number of poppies grows in this field.*

> 1) **untold** 2) **unnamed** 3) **anonymous**

1) *There are **untold** treasures buried at sea.*
2) *The actor got a letter from an **unnamed** admirer.*
3) *My favorite poem is by an **anonymous** writer.*

Opposite: **known**

untidy adjective

If something is **untidy**, it is in a mess.
*Cliff was told to straighten up his **untidy** room.*

> 1) **cluttered** 2) **sloppy** 3) **messy** 3) **chaotic**

1) *Our attic is **cluttered** with old junk.*
2) *The **sloppy** boy was told to get cleaned up.*
3) *Ginny had to explain why her work was **messy**.*
4 *The playroom was **chaotic** after the birthday party.*

Opposites: **neat, tidy**

upset adjective

To be **upset** means to be unhappy because of something
that has happened.
*Lindsay was **upset** when she lost her favorite necklace.*

> 1) **sad** 2) **dismayed** 3) **troubled**

1) *The film made the young children **sad**.*
2) *We were **dismayed** when our house burned down.*
3) *"I am **troubled** to hear such bad news," said the businessman.*

Opposites: **happy, pleased**

urge noun

An **urge** is a strong feeling of wanting to do something.
*When I saw Lizzie yawn, I had an **urge** to yawn, too.*

> 1) **need** 2) **desire** 3) **longing**

1) *The itchy flea bite gave me the **need** to scratch.*
2) *I had a real **desire** to visit my cousin in the Bahamas.*
3) *After waiting for 12 hours, the tired passengers had a **longing** for sleep.*

urgent adjective

Something **urgent** needs attention right away.
*The nurse got an **urgent** message to call the hospital.*

> 1) **important** 2) **crucial** 3) **pressing**

1) *My parents got an **important** letter from the principal.*
2) *It's **crucial** to see a doctor if you think you have appendicitis.*
3) *The executive had to rush because she had a **pressing** appointment.*

use verb

To **use** something means to put it into action.
*You **use** a pen to write a letter.*

> 1) **employ** 2) **utilize** 3) **wield**

1) *We **employed** our brains to solve the mystery.*
2) *She **utilized** a mop to clean the floor.*
3) *You **wield** an ax to chop wood.*

useful adjective

If something is **useful**, it helps you or has value.
*Dad bought a **useful** spray attachment for the garden hose.*

> 1) **practical** 2) **handy** 3) **helpful**

1) *An umbrella is **practical** in the rain.*
2) *Dad got some **handy** hints about looking after his car.*
3) *Mom thanked Gilbert for being a **helpful** boy.*

Opposite: **useless**

useless adjective

If something is **useless**, it has no purpose or meaning.
*The hairbrush was **useless** to the bald man.*

> 1) **pointless** 2) **worthless** 3) **futile**

1) *It was **pointless** to keep the broken toys.*
2) *The flashlight was **worthless** without batteries.*
3) *"It is **futile** to try to escape," said the guard.*

Opposite: **useful**

usual adjective

If something is **usual**, it is normal or typical.
*Dad bought his **usual** newspaper from the shop.*

> 1) **routine** 2) **customary** 3) **regular**

1) *We were asked the **routine** questions.*
2) *The director sat in his **customary** chair.*
3) *Grant went on his **regular** evening walk.*

Opposite: **unusual**

vain adjective

If you are **vain**, you think too highly of yourself.
*Betty was **vain** about her appearance.*

> 1) **conceited** 2) **proud** 3) **self-important**

1) *Brian was **conceited** about his soccer skills.*
2) *Margaret was **proud** of her long, blond hair.*
3) *The mayor was a **self-important** man.*

Opposite: **modest**

valuable adjective

If something is **valuable**, it is important or worth lots of money.
*The British crown jewels are very **valuable**.*

> 1) **costly** 2) **precious** 3) **prized** 3) **treasured**

1) *The **costly** ruby necklace sparkled.*
2) *A rival company stole the **precious** documents.*
3) *Emeralds are highly **prized** jewels.*
4) *My grandfather's watch is my most **treasured** possession.*

Opposite: **worthless**

vanish verb

To **vanish** means to disappear.
*At the end of the show the magician made
the rabbit **vanish**.*

> 1) **disappear** 2) **evaporate** 3) **fade away**

1) *Wizard William could make anything **disappear**.*
2) *The water **evaporated** in the hot sunshine.*
3) *My face cream made my blemishes **fade away**.*

Opposite: **appear**

vast adverb

Something that is **vast** is extremely big.
*America's prairies cover a **vast** area.*

1) **huge** 2) **immense** 3) **enormous** 4) **limitless**

1) *The white rhinoceros has a **huge** horn.*
2) *We saw some **immense** temples in India.*
3) *The university has an **enormous** amount of research money.*
4) *Outer space is **limitless**.*

Opposite: **tiny**

vegetable noun

A **vegetable** is a plant you can eat.
*The farm store sells lots of different **vegetables**.*

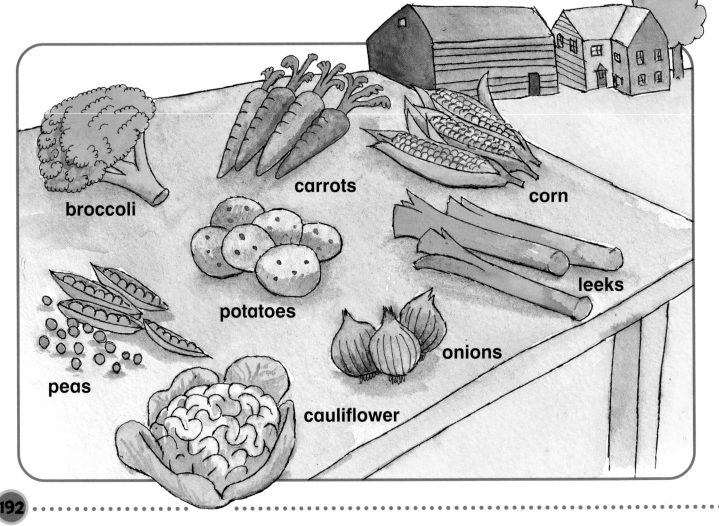

broccoli

carrots

corn

potatoes

leeks

peas

onions

cauliflower

very adverb

Very means to a great degree.
*The winner of the race ran **very** fast.*

1) **absolutely** 2) **exceedingly** 3) **extremely** 4) **particularly**

1) *The soprano sang **absolutely** beautifully at the concert.*
2) *My sister works **exceedingly** hard at school.*
3) *Josh was **extremely** lucky to win the prize.*
4) *The editor wrote **particularly** neatly.*

Opposites: **hardly, slightly**

view noun

The **view** is what you can see from where you are.
*The **view** from the hotel bedroom is lovely.*

1) **scene** 2) **vista** 3) **outlook**

1) *The artist painted the mountain **scene**.*
2) *A **vista** of flowers lay in front of us.*
3) *"What a nice **outlook**!" said the guide.*

viewer noun

A **viewer** is someone who watches.
*The TV star was liked by the **viewers**.*

1) **watcher** 2) **observer** 3) **spectator** 4) **onlooker**

1) *The bird **watcher** observed the bluejays through his binoculars.*
2) *The new employee was an **observer** at the important meeting.*
3) *The **spectators** enjoyed the tennis match.*
4) *Several **onlookers** watched as the firefighters tackled the blaze.*

violent adjective

To be **violent** means to use a lot of force or strength.
*The **violent** wind blew the roof off the house.*

> 1) **savage**   2) **fiery**   3) **raging**   4) **brutal**

1) *We wore hats because of the **savage** heat of the sun.*
2) *The champion boxer had a **fiery** temper.*
3) *The **raging** ocean pounded the shore.*
4) *The **brutal** tiger attacked its prey.*

Opposites: **calm, gentle, peaceful**

visible adjective

If something is **visible**, it can be seen.
*The star's mansion was **visible** in the distance.*

> 1) **noticeable**   2) **clear**   3) **apparent**   4) **in view**

1) *The batter had a **noticeable** bruise on his arm.*
2) *Babies sometimes have **clear** birthmarks.*
3) *The man's surprise was **apparent** on his face.*
4) *My presents were **in view** on the table.*

Opposite: **invisible**

visit verb

To **visit** means to go to see someone or something.
*Dad took us to **visit** the city zoo.*

> 1) **call on**   2) **go to see**   3) **look up**

1) *"Don't forget to **call on** Grandpa," said Mom.*
2) *We **go to see** our cousins once a year.*
3) *The former student went to **look up** his old friends.*

visit noun

A **visit** is a trip to see someone or a short stay in a place.
*Grandma went on a **visit** to her sister's house.*

> 1) **vacation** 2) **trip** 3) **outing**

1) *Our **vacation** at the beach was lots of fun.*
2) *"I am going on a **trip** to Australia," said Vincent.*
3) *The class went on an **outing** to the museum.*

visitor noun

A **visitor** is someone who visits a place or a person.
*The **visitors** were given a guided tour.*

> 1) **caller** 2) **company** 3) **guest** 4) **tourist**

1) *They had lots of **callers** when the baby was born.*
2) *"I enjoy having **company**," said Aunt Beatrice.*
3) *The **guests** were given the best rooms.*
4) *Every summer the city is filled with **tourists**.*

vivid adjective

Something that is **vivid** is very strong and colorful.
*The artist painted a **vivid** portrait of my great-uncle.*

> 1) **brilliant** 2) **bright** 3) **dazzling**

1) *Every year I look forward to seeing the **brilliant** autumn leaves.*
2) *Our new puppy has **bright** green eyes.*
3) *The car's headlights were **dazzling**.*

Opposites: **dull, pale**

wait verb

To **wait** means to stay in one place or do nothing until something happens.
*I **wait** for the school bus on the corner.*

> 1) **linger** 2) **loiter** 3) **remain**

1) *The gardener did not want to **linger** in the cold.*
2) *The lazy boy **loitered** outside the school gate.*
3) *I **remained** at the house until my friends arrived.*

wake verb

To **wake** means to stop being asleep.
*Kevin has to **wake** at seven o'clock.*

> 1) **rise** 2) **rouse** 3) **stir**

1) *Most farmers have to **rise** before dawn.*
2) *The lazy man did not **rouse** until lunchtime.*
3) *Grandpa was so tired he did not **stir** when the alarm clock went off.*

Opposite: **sleep**

walk verb

To **walk** means to move along on foot.
*Jess likes to **walk** to school.*

> 1) **amble** 2) **hike** 3) **stride** 4) **stroll**

1) *My elderly neighbor likes to **amble** to the coffee shop every morning.*
2) *The family **hikes** five miles every Sunday.*
3) *My dad **strides** very fast.*
4) *"Let's go for a **stroll**," suggested Theo.*

wander verb

To **wander** means to move around with no purpose.
*The girls **wander** around the mall on Saturday.*

> 1) **roam** 2) **meander** 3) **drift** 4) **rove**

1) *The traveler had **roamed** all over Europe.*
2) *Zack and I **meandered** through the fairground.*
3) *The lonely boy **drifted** around the city center.*
4) *The hunters **roved** through the forest.*

want verb

To **want** something means to wish to have it.
*She **wants** a new dress for the school dance.*

> 1) **desire** 2) **crave** 3) **long for**

1) *"I **desire** to speak to you," said the principal.*
2) *The miserable children **craved** some fun.*
3) *The wet campers **longed for** a sunny day.*

warm adjective

If something is **warm**, it is of medium heat.
*The bus driver wears a **warm** coat in the winter.*

> 1) **balmy** 2) **heated** 3) **tepid**

1) *It was such a **balmy** day that we decided to sit by the pool.*
2) *The water in the swimming pool was **heated**.*
3) *Edna washed her woolen sweater in **tepid** water.*

Opposite: **cool**

wash verb

To **wash** something means to clean it with water.
*Dad had to **wash** Sam's softball jersey.*

> 1) **bathe** 2) **clean** 3) **launder** 4) **rinse**

1) *I had to **bathe** our smelly dog.*
2) *Dad decided to **clean** the fish tank.*
3) *You can **launder** clothes at a laundromat.*
4) *Kendra **rinsed** her muddy hands under the faucet.*

waste verb

To **waste** something means to use it up carelessly.
*The governor told people not to **waste** water.*

> 1) **throw away** 2) **fritter away** 3) **squander**

1) *The boys **throw away** their money on silly games.*
2) *"Don't **fritter away** your allowance," said Dad.*
3) *Tamara **squandered** her time at school.*

Opposite: **save**

watch verb

To **watch** something means to look at it.
*"I don't want to **watch** TV," said Samantha.*

> 1) **observe** 2) **view** 3) **stare at** 4) **gaze**

1) *Daniel **observed** the football game.*
2) *We wanted to **view** the race.*
3) *"Don't **stare at** me," said the injured boy*
4) *I saw a large tanker as I **gazed** out to sea.*

wave verb

To **wave** means to move from side to side or up and down.
*The flags **wave** in the gentle breeze.*

> 1) **flutter** 2) **flap** 3) **sway**

1) *The sheets **flutter** on the clothesline.*
2) *"Don't **flap** the newspaper around," said Dad.*
3) *The young trees **swayed** in the storm.*

way noun

A **way** of doing something is a method of doing it.
*There are lots of **ways** to cook eggs.*

> 1) **method** 2) **manner** 3) **fashion**

1) *The children learned a new **method** of tying their shoelaces.*
2) *The salesclerk spoke in a rude **manner**.*
3) *My grandmother writes in an odd **fashion**.*

weak adjective

Someone or something that is **weak** has very little strength.
*I am strong but my younger brother is **weak**.*

> 1) **feeble** 2) **delicate** 3) **frail** 4) **puny**

1) *The sick man was too **feeble** to get out of bed.*
2) *My brother was **delicate** when he was young.*
3) *The **frail** old man walked with a cane.*
4) *Our dog was **puny** when he was a puppy.*

Opposite: **strong**

weather noun

The **weather** is the state of the air outside.
*In the summer the **weather** can be hot and sunny.*

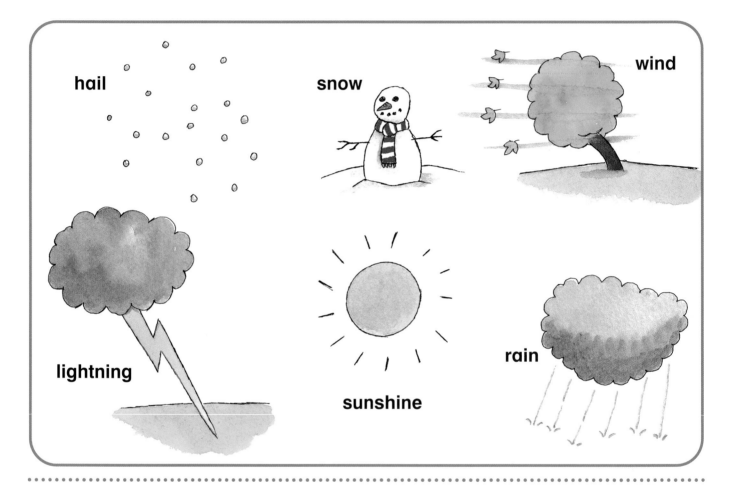

hail

snow

wind

lightning

sunshine

rain

weird adjective

If something is **weird**, it is strange or unusual.
*The artist's house was a **weird** shape.*

1) **strange** 2) **peculiar** 3) **odd** 4) **unusual**

1) *I saw a **strange** picture on the wall.*
2) *The spicy food tasted **peculiar**.*
3) *"You look really **odd**," said my best friend.*
4) *The movie star wore **unusual** clothes.*

Opposites: **usual, normal**

welcome adjective

If something is **welcome**, it is received gladly.
*The hotel guest felt very **welcome**.*

> 1) **acceptable** 2) **wanted** 3) **pleasant**

1) *"This is an **acceptable** idea," said Professor Lau.*
2) *Our new kitten is a **wanted** addition to our home.*
3) *I got a **pleasant** surprise in the mail today.*

Opposites: **unwanted, unwelcome**

well adjective

If you are **well**, you are healthy.
*The doctor told me I was **well**.*

> 1) **fit** 2) **thriving** 3) **healthy**

1) *Olympic athletes have to be very **fit**.*
2) *"Your dog is **thriving**," said the vet.*
3) *Our local farmer always looks **healthy**.*

Opposites: **ill, sick, unwell**

well adverb

If something is done **well**, it is done in a good way.
*The book on the sights of Rome was **well** written.*

> 1) **agreeably** 2) **acceptably** 3) **properly**

1) *The students promised to behave **agreeably**.*
2) *"You have done your work **acceptably**," said Mr. Dixon.*
3) *The tour guide liked to do her job **properly**.*

Opposite: **badly**

wet adjective

To be **wet** means to be covered with liquid.
*Jason hung the **wet** laundry on the line.*

> 1) **moist** 2) **soggy** 3) **soaking** 4) **sopping**

1) *The dog's nose was **moist**.*
2) *I pulled the **soggy** book out of the water.*
3) *"You're **soaking**!" cried Mom when I came in from the rain.*
4) *He put the **sopping** clothes into the dryer.*

Opposite: **dry**

whisper verb

To **whisper** means to speak in a soft voice.
*I was not even allowed to **whisper**.*

> 1) **murmur** 2) **sigh** 3) **hiss**

1) *The assistant **murmured** the answer into his ear.*
2) *The teacher **sighed** my name.*
3) *"Turn the light off!" **hissed** Connie.*

whole adjective

If something is **whole**, it has nothing left out.
*Michael wanted to eat the **whole** apple pie.*

> 1) **entire** 2) **total** 3) **full** 4) **complete**

1) *"I have finished the **entire** book,"
boasted my sister.*
2) *The cashier wanted the **total** amount.*
3) *I wanted Dad to read the **full** story.*
4) *We spent a **complete** day in silence.*

Opposite: **partial**

wicked adjective

To be **wicked** means to be very bad.
*The **wicked** witch mixed up a potion.*

> 1) **heartless** 2) **fiendish** 3) **evil**

1) *A **heartless** thief stole the old man's life savings.*
2) *The **fiendish** pirate attacked the ship.*
3) *The cruel dictator had an **evil** plan.*

Opposites: **good, harmless**

wide adjective

If something is **wide** it measures a long way from one side to the other.
*The presenter of the new game show wore **wide** trousers.*

> 1) **large** 2) **broad** 3) **vast**

1) *The dog escaped through a **large** gap in the fence.*
2) *The giant had **broad** shoulders.*
3) *The fleet of ships sailed down the **vast** river.*

Opposite: **narrow**

wild adjective

If something is **wild**, it lives freely.
*In the nature reserve we saw lots of **wild** animals.*

> 1) **untamed** 2) **feral** 3) **free**

1) *The **untamed** horse could not be ridden.*
2) *There is a **feral** cat living in the woods.*
3) *I wanted the circus animals to be **free**.*

Opposite: **tame**

win verb

To **win** means to finish first in a game or competition.
Debbie was pleased to win the sack race.

> 1) **triumph** 2) **come in first** 3) **succeed**

1) *The girls' team **triumphed** in the basketball competition.*
2) *Jamie **came in first** in the 100-yard dash.*
3) *Everyone tried to beat the last year's winner, but he **succeeded**.*

Opposite: **lose**

wind noun

Wind is a current of air.
*The **wind** blew my umbrella inside out.*

> 1) **breeze** 2) **draft** 3) **gust**

1) *A **breeze** made the flowers move.*
2) *The **draft** came in through the window.*
3) *Robbie felt a cold **gust** on his neck.*

wind verb

To **wind** something means to turn or coil it.
*Dad **winds** the hose up after he has used it.*

> 1) **bend** 2) **twist** 3) **curve**

1) *I tried to **bend** the wire around my finger.*
2) *The climber **twisted** the rope around his waist.*
3) *"The road **curves** to the left," said the driver.*

Opposite: **straighten**

winner noun

The **winner** is the person who wins a contest or battle.
*Mom was the **winner** of the chess game.*

> 1) **victor** 2) **champion** 3) **conqueror**

1) *"Three cheers for the **victor**!" cheered the umpire.*
2) *Stephen had run fastest, so he was the **champion**.*
3) *The battle was over, and the prince was the **conqueror**.*

Opposite: **loser**

woods noun

Woods consist of a large group of trees.
*We went for a stroll in the **woods**.*

> 1) **forest** 2) **copse** 3) **grove**

1) *"I found some acorns in the **forest**," said Nat.*
2) *The **copse** is our favorite place.*
3) *Big apple trees grow in the **grove**.*

work noun

Work is physical or mental effort.
*The delivery man had lots of **work** to do.*

> 1) **labor** 2) **toil** 3) **effort**

1) *Building houses is hard **labor**.*
2) *Ruben's **toil** was rewarded with praise.*
3) *The **effort** made her very tired.*

Opposites: **play, rest**

worry verb

To **worry** means to feel concerned.
*We all started to **worry** about the weather.*

> 1) **fret** 2) **agonize** 3) **be anxious**

1) *We tried not to **fret** about the missing costumes.*
2) *I **agonized** about the terrible secret of my missing brother.*
3) *"Try not to be so **anxious**," said the kind nurse.*

write verb

To **write** means to form words with a pen or pencil, or to create something with words.
*The English students had to **write** a story.*

> 1) **compose** 2) **jot down** 3) **scribble**

1) *Daryl tried to **compose** a thank-you letter.*
2) *Mom said she would **jot down** a shopping list.*
3) *We had to **scribble** some notes in our notebooks.*

wrong adjective

If something is **wrong** it is not correct.
*The dancer put on the **wrong** shoes.*

> 1) **mistaken** 2) **in error** 3) **incorrect**

1) *The clerk said that he had been **mistaken**.*
2) *"I think you are **in error**," said Uncle Pete.*
3) *I gave an **incorrect** answer in our class quiz.*

Opposites: **correct, right**

yell verb

To **yell** means to shout loudly.
*Her little brother **yells** if he doesn't get what he wants.*

> 1) **bawl** 2) **bellow** 3) **scream** 4) **screech**

1) *Babies **bawl** loudly if they get upset.*
2) *The teacher **bellowed** at the noisy children.*
3) *Some people **scream** if you scare them.*
4) *"Do as you are told!" **screeched** the coach.*

Opposite: **whisper**

young adjective

If you are **young** you have only been alive for a short time.
*A kitten is a **young** cat.*

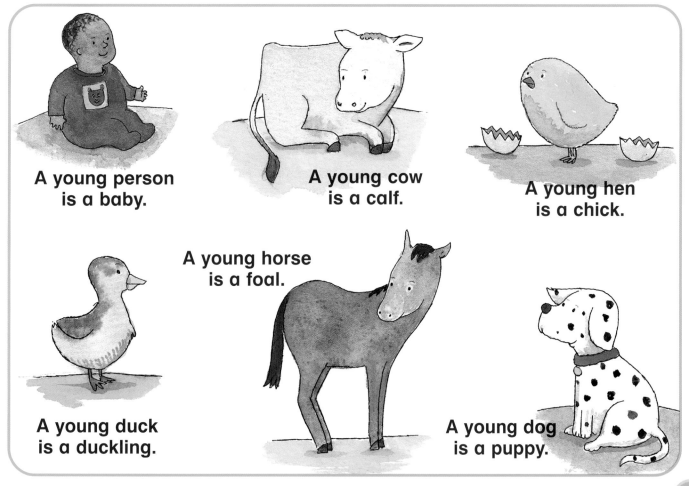

**A young person
is a baby.**

**A young cow
is a calf.**

**A young hen
is a chick.**

**A young horse
is a foal.**

**A young duck
is a duckling.**

**A young dog
is a puppy.**

Zz zero

zero noun

Zero is nothing at all.
*Dan got **zero** on his science test.*

> 1) **nothing** 2) **blank** 3) **naught**

1) *The final score for each team was **nothing**.*
2) *There was a **blank** space on the form.*
3) *His vacation plans came to **naught**.*

zone noun

A **zone** is a place that has a special use.
*We sat in the non-smoking **zone** of the airport.*

> 1) **area** 2) **region** 3) **section**

1) *We parked our car in the blue **area** of the lot.*
2) *She lives in the wine-making **region** of Italy.*
3) *The food **section** of the store was closed.*

zoom verb

To **zoom** is to move very quickly.
*The jet plane **zoomed** overhead.*

> 1) **dart** 2) **dash** 3) **speed**

1) *The dragonfly **darted** across the pond.*
2) *I **dashed** inside when I heard the phone ring.*
3) *The driver tried to **speed** around the track in record time.*

Index

All the headwords and synonyms that appear in the thesaurus are listed in alphabetical order in this index.

When you find a word in the alphabetical list, the headword entry you need to look up is given after the word *see*. For some words, there is more than one headword to look up, for example **admire**.

Where a word or headword is listed more than once, to help you find the right word the different meanings or the parts of speech are given in brackets afterwards: for example, **bad** (naughty) and **bad** (rotten) or **end** (noun) and **end** (verb).

A

a lot of *see* MANY
able *see* ABLE
abode *see* HOME
about *see* ABOUT
above *see* ABOVE
abrupt *see* SUDDEN
absent *see* ABSENT, OUT
absolute *see* TOTAL (adj)
absolutely *see* QUITE, VERY
absurd *see* INCREDIBLE, SILLY
abundant *see* MANY
accept *see* ADMIT, AGREE
acceptable *see* WELCOME
acceptably *see* WELL (adv)
accident *see* ACCIDENT, DISASTER
accompany *see* GUIDE
account *see* STORY
accurate *see* CORRECT, RIGHT
achieve *see* DO
aching *see* PAINFUL
acknowledge *see* ADMIT
acquire *see* GET
act *see* BEHAVE
active *see* ACTIVE, BUSY
actor *see* ACTOR
add *see* ADD, COUNT
additional *see* SPARE
adequate *see* ENOUGH
adjacent *see* NEAR
adjudicator *see* JUDGE (noun)
admire *see* ADMIRE, LIKE (verb),
     RESPECT
admit *see* ADMIT
adore *see* ADMIRE, LOVE
adult *see* ADULT
advertisement *see* NOTICE (noun)
affluent *see* RICH
affordable *see* CHEAP

afraid *see* AFRAID
aged *see* OLD
agonize *see* WORRY
agree *see* AGREE
agreeable *see* NICE
agreeably *see* WELL (adv)
agreement *see* PERMISSION
aid *see* HELP
ailing *see* ILL
aim *see* OBJECT, TRY
aircaft *see* AIRCRAFT
ajar *see* OPEN (adj)
alarm *see* FEAR, FRIGHTEN,
     SCARE
alert *see* ALERT, AWAKE
alight *see* LAND (verb)
alike *see* SAME
all set *see* READY
ally *see* FRIEND
almost *see* ABOUT
alone *see* LONELY
alter *see* CHANGE
amazing *see* EXTRAORDINARY,
     FANTASTIC
amble *see* WALK
amid *see* BETWEEN
among *see* BETWEEN
amount *see* TOTAL (noun)
ample *see* ENOUGH
amusing *see* AMUSING, FUNNY
ancient *see* OLD
angry *see* ANGRY, CROSS
animal *see* ANIMAL, BEAST,
     CREATURE
announce *see* CALL, TELL
annoy *see* ANNOY
annoyed *see* ANGRY, CROSS
anonymous *see* UNKNOWN
answer *see* ANSWER
anxious *see* KEEN, NERVOUS

apologetic *see* SORRY
apparatus *see* MACHINE
apparent *see* VISIBLE
appear *see* APPEAR, COME
appetizing *see* DELICIOUS
appraise *see* JUDGE (verb)
appreciate *see* ENJOY
appreciative *see* THANKFUL
approach *see* COME
approval *see* PERMISSION
approximately *see* ABOUT
area *see* ZONE
argue *see* ARGUE, QUARREL
arid *see* DRY
arise *see* HAPPEN, WAKE
aroma *see* SMELL
arrange *see* ARRANGE,
     ORGANIZE
arrest *see* CATCH
arrive *see* COME, ENTER,
     LAND (verb)
article *see* OBJECT, THING
ascend *see* CLIMB
ashamed *see* SORRY
ashen *see* PALE
ask *see* ASK, INVITE, QUESTION
asleep *see* ASLEEP
assassinate *see* KILL
assemble *see* BUILD, COLLECT,
     MEET
assess *see* JUDGE (verb)
assist *see* HELP
assorted *see* DIFFERENT
at one time *see* ONCE
attempt *see* GO (noun), TRY
attentive *see* ALERT, AWAKE
attract *see* DRAW
attractive *see* BEAUTIFUL,
     HANDSOME,
     LOVELY, PRETTY

Index

Index

deal with *see* TREAT
debris *see* LITTER
deceased *see* DEAD
deceive *see* TRICK
decide *see* DECIDE
decide on *see* PICK
decline *see* REFUSE
decree *see* RULE (noun)
deep *see* THICK
defend *see* PROTECT
definite *see* SURE
delayed *see* LATE
delicate *see* WEAK
delicious *see* DELICIOUS
delighted *see* GLAD, HAPPY
demanding *see* HARD
demolish *see* DESTROY, RUIN
demonstrate *see* EXPLAIN
dense *see* STUPID
deny *see* REFUSE
depart *see* GO (verb), LEAVE
departed *see* DEAD
depend on *see* TRUST
descend *see* FALL
desire *see* LONG FOR, URGE,
　　　　WANT
despise *see* HATE
destitute *see* POOR
destroy *see* DAMAGE, DESTROY,
　　　　RUIN, SPOIL
detect *see* DISCOVER, NOTICE
　　　　(verb)
determine *see* DECIDE
detest *see* DISLIKE, HATE
devastate *see* DAMAGE
develop *see* GROW
device *see* MACHINE
different *see* DIFFERENT
difficult *see* HARD
dig *see* DIG
dignified *see* GRAND
dim *see* DARK, FAINT, STUPID
dinosaur *see* DINOSAUR
direct *see* GUIDE, ORDER
dirty *see* DIRTY
disagree *see* ARGUE, QUARREL
disappear *see* VANISH
disaster *see* ACCIDENT, DISASTER
discover *see* DISCOVER, FIND
dislike *see* DISLIKE, HATE
dismal *see* DULL, UNHAPPY
dismayed *see* UPSET
disobedient *see* NAUGHTY
dispatch *see* SEND

display *see* SHOW
displeased *see* ANGRY
disregard *see* IGNORE
dissolve *see* MELT
distant *see* FARAWAY
distribute *see* SHARE
dive *see* DIVE, FALL
divide *see* SHARE
do *see* DO
dodge *see* MISS
donate *see* GIVE
donation *see* GIFT
doodle *see* DRAW
dote on *see* LOVE
doubt *see* DOUBT
downcast *see* UNHAPPY
downpour *see* RAIN
doze *see* SLEEP
dozing *see* ASLEEP
drab *see* DULL
draft *see* WIND (noun)
drag *see* PULL
draw (attract) *see* DRAW
draw (sketch) *see* DRAW
dread *see* FEAR
dreadful *see* HORRIBLE
dreary *see* BORING, DULL
drift *see* WANDER
drivel *see* NONSENSE
drizzle *see* RAIN
drop *see* DIVE, FALL, LOSE
drop by *see* CALL
dry *see* DRY
dull (boring) *see* BORING, DULL
dull (cloudy) *see* DULL
dutiful *see* OBEDIENT
dwelling *see* HOME

E

eager *see* EAGER, KEEN
earlier *see* OLD
earn *see* GET
earth *see* LAND (noun)
easy *see* EASY, SIMPLE
eat *see* EAT
edgy *see* NERVOUS
effort *see* GO (noun), WORK
elderly *see* OLD
elect *see* CHOOSE
elevate *see* RAISE
elsewhere *see* OUT
eminent *see* FAMOUS
employ *see* USE

emptiness *see* NOTHING
empty *see* EMPTY
end (noun) *see* END (noun)
end (verb) *see* END (verb), FINISH
ended *see* OVER
ending *see* END (noun)
endless *see* LONG (adj)
endure *see* LAST (verb)
energetic *see* ACTIVE
enigma *see* MYSTERY
enjoy *see* ENJOY, LIKE (verb)
enjoyable *see* AMUSING
enormous *see* BIG, ENORMOUS,
　　　　GREAT, LARGE,
　　　　VAST
enough *see* ENOUGH
ensemble *see* BAND
enter *see* ENTER
entertaining *see* FUNNY
enthusiastic *see* EAGER, KEEN
entice *see* DRAW
entire *see* COMPLETE, WHOLE
entirety *see* TOTAL (noun)
envious *see* JEALOUS
equal *see* EVEN, FAIR
error *see* MISTAKE
escalate *see* RAISE
escort *see* LEAD
estimate *see* GUESS
evade *see* MISS
evaluate *see* JUDGE (verb)
evaporate *see* VANISH
even (flat) *see* EVEN
even (the same) *see* EVEN
everyday *see* ORDINARY
evil *see* BAD, EVIL, WICKED
exact *see* PERFECT, RIGHT
examine *see* CHECK, LOOK
excavate *see* DIG
exceedingly *see* VERY
excellent *see* EXCELLENT, GOOD,
　　　　IDEAL, PERFECT
excited *see* EXCITED
exclaim *see* SAY
excursion *see* JOURNEY
execute *see* KILL
exhausted *see* TIRED
expedition *see* JOURNEY, QUEST
experience *see* KNOWLEDGE
explain *see* EXPLAIN
expose *see* UNCOVER
exquisite *see* LOVELY
extended *see* LONG (adj)
exterior *see* OUTSIDE

external *see* OUTSIDE
extinct *see* EXTINCT
extra *see* SPARE
extraordinary *see*
          EXTRAORDINARY,
          FANTASTIC
extremely *see* VERY

F

fade away *see* VANISH
faint *see* FAINT
fair *see* FAIR
fairy tale *see* STORY
fall *see* FALL
famished *see* HUNGRY
famous *see* FAMOUS
fantastic *see* FANTASTIC
far-fetched *see* FANTASTIC,
          INCREDIBLE
faraway *see* FARAWAY
fascinating *see* INTERESTING
fashion *see* WAY
fashionable *see* MODERN
fast *see* FAST, QUICK
fasten *see* CLOSE
fat *see* FAT
faultless *see* IDEAL, PERFECT
fear *see* FEAR
fearful *see* AFRAID
fearless *see* BRAVE
feast *see* MEAL
feeble *see* WEAK
feel *see* FEEL, TOUCH
feral *see* WILD
ferocious *see* FIERCE
fetch *see* BRING
fiendish *see* WICKED
fierce *see* FIERCE
fiery *see* VIOLENT
fight *see* FIGHT, QUARREL
file *see* MARCH
fill *see* FILL
filled *see* FULL
film *see* LAYER
filthy *see* DIRTY
final *see* LAST (adj)
find *see* DISCOVER, FIND
fine *see* BEAUTIFUL, HANDSOME
finger *see* FEEL
finish *see* END (noun), END (verb),
          FINISH, STOP
finished *see* OVER
firm *see* CRISP, HARD, STRICT

first class *see* GOOD
fit *see* WELL (adj)
fitter *see* BETTER
fitting *see* PROPER
fix *see* FIX, MEND
flame *see* BURN
flap *see* WAVE
flare *see* BURN
flat *see* EVEN
flatten *see* CRUSH
flawless *see* PERFECT
flexible *see* SOFT
flimsy *see* LIGHT (adj)
fling *see* THROW
float *see* FLY
flutter *see* WAVE
fly *see* FLY, RUSH
fog *see* FOG
follow *see* FOLLOW
following *see* NEXT
food *see* FOOD
fool *see* TRICK
foolish *see* SILLY, STUPID
foot *see* BOTTOM
force *see* MAKE
forest *see* WOODS
forget *see* FORGET
forgetful *see* CARELESS
former *see* OLD
formerly *see* ONCE
forsaken *see* LONELY
fortune *see* TREASURE
forward *see* SEND
fountain *see* JET
fracture *see* BREAK (verb)
fragment *see* BIT, PART
fragrance *see* SMELL
frail *see* WEAK
free *see* FREE, RESCUE, WILD
free (available) *see* FREE
free (complimentary) *see* FREE
freezing *see* COLD
frequently *see* OFTEN
fresh *see* CLEAN, NEW
fret *see* WORRY
friend *see* FRIEND
friendless *see* LONELY
fright *see* FEAR
frighten *see* FRIGHTEN
frightened *see* AFRAID
fritter away *see* WASTE
frolic *see* PLAY
frosty *see* COLD
frown *see* FROWN

fruit *see* FRUIT
full *see* COMPLETE, FULL, WHOLE
full grown *see* ADULT
fully *see* QUITE
funds *see* MONEY
funny (amusing) *see* AMUSING,
          FUNNY
funny (odd) *see* FUNNY
furious *see* ANGRY, MAD
fury *see* TEMPER
fuss *see* FUSS
futile *see* USELESS

G

gag *see* JOKE (noun)
gamble *see* RISK
game *see* MATCH
gap *see* BREAK (noun)
gaping *see* OPEN (adj)
garbage *see* LITTER, RUBBISH
gather *see* COLLECT, MEET
gaze *see* LOOK, WATCH
gem *see* JEWEL
gemstone *see* JEWEL
generous *see* GENEROUS
gentle *see* GENTLE, KIND (adj),
          MILD
genuine *see* REAL, TRUE
get *see* GET, UNDERSTAND
get along *see* AGREE
giant *see* ENORMOUS
gibberish *see* NONSENSE
gift *see* GIFT
gigantic *see* ENORMOUS
giggle *see* LAUGH
give *see* GIVE, PASS
glad *see* GLAD
gladden *see* PLEASE
glare *see* FROWN
glaring *see* BRIGHT
gleam *see* SHINE
glide *see* FLY, SLIDE
glimmer *see* GLOW
glimpse *see* SEE
glitter *see* SHINE
gloat *see* BOAST
gloomy *see* DARK, DULL
glorious *see* GRAND
glossy *see* SMOOTH
glow *see* GLOW
glower *see* FROWN
gluttonous *see* GREEDY
go (noun) *see* GO (noun)

Index

interesting *see* INTERESTING
interior *see* INSIDE
intermission *see* BREAK (noun)
internal *see* INSIDE
interrogate *see* ASK,
     QUESTION
intriguing *see* INTERESTING
invisible *see* INVISIBLE
invite *see* INVITE
irate *see* MAD
irritate *see* ANNOY
irritated *see* CROSS
irritation *see* NUISANCE
issue *see* MATTER, TOPIC
item *see* OBJECT, THING

J

jealous *see* JEALOUS
jerk *see* JOLT
jest *see* JOKE (noun)
jet *see* JET
jewel *see* JEWEL
job *see* JOB
join *see* JOIN
joke (noun) *see* JOKE (noun)
joke (verb) *see* JOKE (verb)
jolt *see* JOLT, SURPRISE
jostle *see* JOLT
jot down *see* WRITE
journey *see* JOURNEY
joyful *see* GLAD
judge (noun) *see* JUDGE (noun)
judge (verb) *see* JUDGE (verb)
jumble *see* MESS
jump *see* JUMP
just *see* FAIR, ONLY (adv)

K

keen *see* EAGER, KEEN, SHARP
keep *see* KEEP, SAVE
key *see* IMPORTANT
kid *see* KID
kill *see* KILL
killed *see* DEAD
kind (adj) *see* KIND (adj)
kind (noun) *see* KIND (noun),
     SORT
kneel *see* KNEEL
knock *see* KNOCK
knock down *see* DESTROY
knot *see* KNOT
know (identify) *see* KNOW

know (realize) *see* KNOW,
     UNDERSTAND
knowledge *see* KNOWLEDGE

L

labor *see* WORK
land (noun) *see* LAND (noun)
land (verb) *see* LAND (verb)
lanky *see* TALL
large *see* BIG, LARGE, WIDE
last (adj) *see* LAST (adj)
last (verb) *see* LAST (verb)
late *see* LATE
later *see* NEXT
latest *see* MODERN
laugh *see* LAUGH
launder *see* WASH
lavish *see* GENEROUS
law *see* RULE (noun)
lay *see* PLACE (verb)
layer *see* LAYER
laze *see* RELAX
lazy *see* LAZY, SLOW
lead *see* GUIDE, LEAD, RULE
     (verb)
leading *see* IMPORTANT
lean *see* THIN
leap *see* JUMP
leave *see* LEAVE, GO (verb)
leftover *see* SPARE
legend *see* STORY
leisure activity *see* HOBBY
leisurely *see* SLOW
lengthy *see* LONG (adj)
level *see* EVEN
liberal *see* GENEROUS
lie *see* LIE
lifeless *see* DEAD
lift *see* RAISE
light (adj) *see* LIGHT (adj)
light (noun) *see* LIGHT (noun)
lightweight *see* LIGHT (adj)
like (adj) *see* LIKE (adj)
like (verb) *see* ENJOY, LIKE (verb)
limitless *see* VAST
line *see* ROW
linger *see* STAY, WAIT
link *see* JOIN
litter *see* LITTER, RUBBISH
little *see* LITTLE, SHORT, SMALL,
     TINY
lively *see* ACTIVE, EXCITED
load *see* FILL

loathe *see* DISLIKE, HATE
location *see* PLACE (noun)
lock *see* CLOSE
lofty *see* HIGH
loiter *see* WAIT
lone *see* ONLY (adj)
lonely *see* LONELY
long (adj) *see* LONG (adj)
long for *see* LONG FOR, MISS,
     WANT
long-faced *see* SERIOUS
long-suffering *see* PATIENT
longing *see* URGE
look *see* LOOK
look over *see* CHECK
look up *see* VISIT (verb)
loom *see* APPEAR
loop *see* KNOT
lose *see* LOSE
lost *see* EXTINCT
loud *see* LOUD, NOISY
lounge *see* LIE
love *see* ENJOY, LOVE
lovely *see* BEAUTIFUL, LOVELY,
     PRETTY
loving *see* KIND (adj)

M

machine *see* MACHINE
mad *see* MAD
magic *see* MAGIC
magnanimous *see* GENEROUS
mail *see* SEND
main *see* MAIN
majestic *see* GRAND
make (compel) *see* MAKE
make (create) *see* BUILD, COOK,
     MAKE
make clear *see* EXPLAIN
make tracks *see* LEAVE
manner *see* WAY
many *see* MANY
march *see* MARCH
mark *see* MARK
mash *see* CRUSH
massive *see* ENORMOUS, LARGE
match *see* MATCH
matching *see* SAME
matter *see* MATTER
mature *see* ADULT
meal *see* MEAL
mean (adj) *see* MEAN (adj),
     UNKIND

Index

mean (verb) *see* MEAN (verb)
meander *see* WANDER
meek *see* SHY
meet *see* MEET
melt *see* MELT
mend *see* FIX, HEAL, MEND
merely *see* ONLY (adv)
merge *see* MIX
mess *see* MESS
messy *see* CARELESS, UNTIDY
metal *see* METAL
method *see* WAY
middle *see* MIDDLE
mild *see* GENTLE, MILD
mind *see* CARE, MIND
mingle *see* MIX
miniature *see* LITTLE, SMALL
minute *see* LITTLE, TINY
miserable *see* SAD, UNHAPPY
mislay *see* LOSE
misplace *see* LOSE
miss (avoid) *see* MISS
miss (pine) *see* MISS
missing *see* ABSENT
mission *see* QUEST
mist *see* FOG
mistake *see* MISTAKE
mistaken *see* WRONG
mistrust *see* DOUBT
mix *see* MIX
moan *see* MOAN
mock *see* JOKE (verb)
model *see* IDEAL
modern *see* MODERN
modify *see* CHANGE
moist *see* DAMP, WET
moldy *see* BAD
money *see* MONEY
monster *see* BEAST, MONSTER
mope *see* SULK
mound *see* PILE
mountain *see* PILE
move *see* CARRY, MOVE
much *see* OFTEN
muddy *see* DIRTY
mumble *see* MUMBLE
munch *see* EAT
murder *see* KILL
murky *see* DARK
murmur *see* MUMBLE, WHISPER
muse *see* THINK
mutter *see* MUMBLE
mystery *see* MYSTERY

N

naked *see* BARE
nap *see* REST, SLEEP
narrow *see* NARROW
nasty *see* HORRIBLE, MEAN, NASTY, UNKIND
naught *see* ZERO
naughty *see* BAD, NAUGHTY
near *see* NEAR
nearly *see* ABOUT
neat *see* NEAT, TIDY
need *see* NEED, URGE
needy *see* POOR
neighboring *see* NEAR
nervous *see* NERVOUS
new *see* NEW
newborn *see* BABY
next *see* NEXT
nice *see* NICE
noiseless *see* QUIET, SILENT
noisy *see* LOUD, NOISY
nonsense *see* NONSENSE
normal *see* NORMAL, ORDINARY
nosy *see* NOSY
nothing *see* NOTHING, ZERO
notice (noun) *see* NOTICE (noun)
notice (verb) *see* FIND, NOTICE (verb)
noticeable *see* VISIBLE
notify *see* TELL
novel *see* NEW
nude *see* BARE
nuisance *see* NUISANCE
numerous *see* MANY

O

obedient *see* GOOD, OBEDIENT
object (aim) *see* OBJECT
object (article) *see* OBJECT, THING
oblige *see* MAKE
observant *see* ALERT
observe *see* NOTICE (verb), WATCH
observer *see* VIEWER
obtain *see* GET
obvious *see* CLEAR
occupation *see* JOB
occupied *see* BUSY
occur *see* HAPPEN
odd *see* FUNNY, ODD, STRANGE, WEIRD
odor *see* SMELL

often *see* OFTEN
old (aged) *see* OLD
old (earlier) *see* OLD
omit *see* FORGET
on the house *see* FREE
on top of *see* ABOVE
once *see* ONCE
one-sided *see* UNFAIR
onlooker *see* VIEWER
only (adj) *see* ONLY (adj)
only (adv) *see* ONLY (adv)
open (adj) *see* OPEN (adj)
open (verb) *see* OPEN (verb), START, UNDO, UNFOLD
opening *see* START
opposite *see* DIFFERENT
opt for *see* PICK
orchestra *see* BAND
order *see* ORDER
orderly *see* NEAT, TIDY
ordinary *see* NORMAL, ORDINARY
organize *see* ARRANGE, ORGANIZE
original *see* NEW
out *see* OUT
out of the question *see* IMPOSSIBLE
outdo *see* PASS
outdoor *see* OUTSIDE
outing *see* VISIT (noun)
outlook *see* VIEW
outlying *see* FARAWAY
outside *see* OUTSIDE
outstanding *see* EXCELLENT
outstrip *see* PASS
over *see* ABOVE, OVER
overdue *see* LATE
overlook *see* FORGET, IGNORE
oversight *see* MISTAKE
overweight *see* FAT
own *see* HAVE
own up *see* ADMIT

P

pack *see* FILL
packed *see* FULL
pain *see* NUISANCE
painful *see* PAINFUL
pal *see* FRIEND
pale *see* FAINT, PALE
parade *see* MARCH
parched *see* DRY

Index

reserve *see* KEEP
residence *see* HOME
resolve *see* DECIDE
respect *see* RESPECT
respectful *see* OBEDIENT
respond *see* ANSWER, BEHAVE
rest (nap) *see* BREAK (noun),
            PLACE (verb),
            RELAX, REST
rest (remainder) *see* REST
restful *see* PEACEFUL
retain *see* KEEP
retort *see* ANSWER
reveal *see* SHOW, UNCOVER
revere *see* RESPECT
revolve *see* SPIN, TURN
rich *see* RICH
riches *see* MONEY, TREASURE
riddle *see* MYSTERY
ridicule *see* JOKE (verb)
right *see* CORRECT, FAIR, RIGHT
rigid *see* HARD
ring *see* BAND
rinse *see* WASH
rip *see* TEAR
rise *see* WAKE
risk *see* DANGER, RISK
roam *see* WANDER
roar *see* SHOUT
roast *see* BAKE
rock *see* JEWEL
romp *see* PLAY
rotate *see* TURN
rotten *see* BAD
rough *see* ROUGH
roughly *see* ABOUT
round *see* ROUND
rouse *see* WAKE
routine *see* USUAL
rove *see* WANDER
row *see* ROW
rubbish *see* RUBBISH
rude *see* RUDE
ruin *see* DAMAGE, DESTROY,
        HARM, RUIN, SPOIL
rule (noun) *see* RULE (noun)
rule (verb) *see* RULE (verb)
rumor *see* RUMOR
run *see* ORGANIZE, RULE (verb),
        RUN
run after *see* CHASE
rush *see* HURRY, RUSH, SPEED
ruthless *see* CRUEL

S

sad *see* SAD, UNHAPPY, UPSET
safe *see* SAFE
salvage *see* RESCUE
same *see* EVEN, SAME
satisfied *see* CERTAIN, PROUD
satisfy *see* PLEASE
savage *see* FIERCE, VIOLENT
save *see* COLLECT, KEEP,
        RESCUE, SAVE
say *see* SAY
scalding *see* HOT
scamper *see* RUN
scare *see* FRIGHTEN, SCARE
scared *see* AFRAID
scene *see* VIEW
scent *see* SMELL
scoop *see* DIG
scorching *see* HOT
scoured *see* CLEAN
scowl *see* FROWN, SULK
scramble *see* RUSH
scrap *see* PIECE
scream *see* SCREAM, YELL
screech *see* SCREAM, YELL
scribble *see* WRITE
scrumptious *see* DELICIOUS
scurry *see* HURRY
seat *see* SEAT
secret *see* SECRET
secrete *see* HIDE
section *see* ZONE
secure *see* KNOT, SAFE
see *see* KNOW, SEE
seething *see* MAD
segment *see* PART, PIECE
seize *see* GRAB, TAKE
select *see* CHOOSE, PICK
self-centered *see* SELFISH
self-important *see* VAIN
selfish *see* GREEDY, MEAN (adj),
        SELFISH
send *see* SEND
sensible *see* SENSIBLE
serene *see* CALM, MILD,
        PEACEFUL
serious *see* SERIOUS
set off *see* GO (verb)
set out *see* LEAVE
set up *see* START
settle *see* STAY
severe *see* STRICT
shade *see* COLOR

shadowy *see* DARK
shake *see* JOLT, SHAKE
shambles *see* MESS
shape *see* SHAPE
share *see* SHARE
sharp *see* ALERT, SHARP
shatter *see* BREAK (verb)
sheet *see* LAYER
shelter *see* PROTECT
shield *see* PROTECT
shine *see* GLOW, SHINE
shiny *see* BRIGHT, SMOOTH
shiver *see* SHAKE
shock *see* SURPRISE
shoe *see* SHOE
short *see* SHORT
shout *see* CALL, SHOUT
shove *see* PUSH
show *see* SHOW
show off *see* BOAST
shower *see* RAIN
shriek *see* SCREAM
shudder *see* SHAKE
shut *see* CLOSE
shy *see* SHY
sick *see* ILL
side with *see* AGREE
sigh *see* WHISPER
sign *see* NOTICE (noun)
significant *see* SPECIAL
signify *see* MEAN (verb)
silent *see* QUIET, SILENT
silliness *see* NONSENSE
silly *see* SILLY
similar to *see* LIKE (adj)
simple *see* CLEAR, EASY, SIMPLE
sincere *see* REAL
skate *see* SLIDE
sketch *see* DRAW
skid *see* SLIDE
skillful *see* ABLE
skinny *see* THIN
slam *see* CLOSE
slay *see* KILL
sleek *see* SMOOTH
sleep *see* REST, SLEEP
sleeping *see* ASLEEP
sleepy *see* TIRED
slender *see* NARROW, THIN
slice *see* CUT
slide *see* SLIDE
slight *see* LIGHT
slim *see* NARROW, THIN
slip *see* SLIDE

Index

thankful *see* THANKFUL
thaw *see* MELT
theme *see* TOPIC
theory *see* IDEA
thick *see* THICK
thin *see* NARROW, THIN
thing *see* OBJECT, THING
think *see* GUESS, THINK
thirsty *see* DRY
thoughtless *see* CARELESS
threat *see* DANGER
thrill *see* PLEASE
thrilled *see* EXCITED, HAPPY
thriving *see* WELL (adj)
throbbing *see* PAINFUL
throw *see* THROW
throw away *see* WASTE
thrust *see* PUSH
thud *see* THUD
thump *see* HIT, THUD
thunderous *see* LOUD
tidy *see* NEAT, TIDY
tie *see* KNOT
tight *see* TIGHT
timid *see* NERVOUS, SHY
tint *see* COLOR
tiny *see* LITTLE, SMALL, TINY
tip *see* TOP
tired *see* TIRED
toddler *see* BABY, CHILD, KID
toil *see* WORK
tool *see* MACHINE, TOOL
top *see* TOP
topic *see* MATTER, TOPIC
toss *see* THROW
total (adj) *see* COMPLETE, TOTAL
       (adj), WHOLE
total (noun) *see* TOTAL (noun)
total (verb) *see* ADD, COUNT
totally *see* ONLY, QUITE
touch *see* FEEL, TOUCH
touch down *see* LAND (verb)
tough *see* HARD, TOUGH,
       STRONG
tourist *see* VISITOR
tow *see* PULL
towering *see* HIGH, TALL
trace *see* DRAW, FIND
track *see* CHASE, FOLLOW
trail *see* FOLLOW
transfer *see* MOVE, PASS
transform *see* CHANGE
transmit *see* SEND
transparent *see* CLEAR

transport *see* CARRY
trap *see* CATCH, TRAP
trash *see* LITTER
travel *see* TRAVEL
treasure *see* TREASURE
treasured *see* VALUABLE
treat *see* TREAT
trek *see* JOURNEY
tremble *see* SHAKE
trick *see* TRICK
trim *see* CUT, NEAT
trip *see* JOURNEY, VISIT (noun)
triumph *see* WIN
troop *see* MARCH
trouble *see* FUSS, PROBLEM
troubled *see* UPSET
true *see* CORRECT, REAL, TRUE
trust *see* TRUST
try *see* GO (noun), TRY
tubby *see* FAT
tug *see* PULL
tunnel *see* DIG
turn (noun) *see* BEND (noun)
turn (verb) *see* BEND (verb),
            TURN (verb)
turn a blind eye *see* IGNORE
turn up *see* APPEAR
tutor *see* TEACHER
twirl *see* SPIN
twist *see* BEND (noun)
twist *see* BEND (verb), WIND (verb)
type *see* KIND (noun), SORT

U

ugly *see* AWFUL, UGLY
umpire *see* JUDGE (noun)
unachievable *see* IMPOSSIBLE
unattractive *see* UGLY
unbutton *see* UNDO
unclouded *see* CLEAR
uncomplaining *see* PATIENT
uncork *see* OPEN (verb)
uncover *see* DISCOVER,
         UNCOVER
under *see* UNDER
underneath *see* UNDER
understand *see* KNOW,
         UNDERSTAND
understanding *see* KNOWLEDGE
undetectable *see* INVISIBLE
undo *see* UNDO
undressed *see* BARE
unearth *see* DISCOVER

uneasy *see* NERVOUS
unexpected *see* SUDDEN
unfair *see* UNFAIR
unfasten *see* OPEN (verb)
unfold *see* UNFOLD
unfreeze *see* MELT
unfriendly *see* MEAN
unfurl *see* UNFOLD
ungenerous *see* SELFISH
unhappy *see* SAD, UNHAPPY
unharmed *see* SAFE
uninteresting *see* BORING, DULL
unique *see* SPECIAL
unite *see* JOIN
unjust *see* UNFAIR
unkind *see* NASTY, UNKIND
unknown *see* SECRET, UNKNOWN
unlocked *see* OPEN (adj)
unmask *see* UNCOVER
unnamed *see* UNKNOWN
unoccupied *see* EMPTY, FREE
unpleasant *see* AWFUL,
          HORRIBLE
untamed *see* WILD
untidy *see* UNTIDY
untie *see* UNDO
untiring *see* PATIENT
untold *see* UNKNOWN
unusual *see* EXTRAORDINARY,
         FUNNY, WEIRD
unwell *see* ILL
unwind *see* RELAX
unwise *see* SILLY
unwrap *see* OPEN (verb)
unyielding *see* HARD
upon *see* ABOVE
uproar *see* FUSS
upset *see* UPSET
urge *see* URGE
urgent *see* IMPORTANT, URGENT
use *see* TREAT, USE
useful *see* USEFUL
useless *see* USELESS
usher *see* GUIDE, LEAD
usual *see* NORMAL, USUAL
utilize *see* USE
utter *see* SAY, TOTAL (adj)

V

vacant *see* EMPTY, FREE
vacation *see* VISIT (noun)
vain *see* VAIN
valuable *see* VALUABLE